Spiritual Mind

Without Having a Spiritual Mind
There Can Never Be a True Christian Life

By Pastor Dr. Endiryas Hawaz

TRILOGY

Spiritual Mind: Without Having a Spiritual Mind There Can Never Be a True Christian Life

Trilogy Christian Publishers A Wholly Owned Subsidiary of Trinity Broadcasting Network

2442 Michelle Drive Tustin, CA 92780

Rights Department, 2442 Michelle Drive, Tustin, CA 92780.

Trilogy Christian Publishing/TBN and colophon are trademarks of Trinity Broadcasting Network.

Cover design by: Birukyihun Shigute

Proofreading by: Dr. Annette Cederhole Ed.D

For information about special discounts for bulk purchases, please contact Trilogy Christian Publishing.

Trilogy Disclaimer: The views and content expressed in this book are those of the author and may not necessarily reflect the views and doctrine of Trilogy Christian Publishing or the Trinity Broadcasting Network.

10 9 8 7 6 5 4 3 2 1

Library of Congress Cataloging-in-Publication Data is available.

ISBN: 979-8-89041-242-3

E-ISBN: 979-8-89041-243-0

It was the famed preacher Charles Swindoll who delivered the famous statement on "attitude." He said, "The longer I live, the more I realize the impact of attitude on life... I am convinced that life is 10% what happens to me and 90% how I react to it." Pastor Endiryas Hawaz, in his latest book, "The Spiritual Mind," brings both science and scripture to bear on the topic. He helps the reader understand the power of the mind, often untapped, which determines how an individual approaches life. The mind really does impact the 90%. Led by the Spirit and the Word of God, the mind is able to overcome despair and pain even in overwhelmingly tragic circumstances. In fact, the Spiritual Mind or the "mind of Christ" in us changes our thinking and emotions, which positively impacts our relationships. The Scriptures tell us, "rejoice in the Lord always" (Philippians 4:4). How is this possible in the face of life's daily challenges, pains and conflicts? Pastor Hawaz gives us the answer! His chapters on emotions, meditation, and discipleship are a must read for the Christian who desires the mind of Christ, the Spiritual mind, to shape and form and reform our lives.

Rev. Dr. Peter Meier
Executive Director of Missions and Outreach
The Florida-Georgia District, Lutheran Church – Missouri Synod

I recently had the privilege of reading the book "Spiritual Mind" by Pastor Dr. Endrias Hawaz. Honestly, when I was asked to read it and do a review, I wondered when I would be able to work it into my schedule. However, when I began reading it, I was immediately drawn in by the author's handling of some topics that can be confusing or challenging to explain. In fact, I completed the entire book in just two sittings! I truly appreciate Pastor Dr. Hawaz's research and discussion of topics such as the body, spirit, soul and mind. I do like how he has based his work on God's Word and has further explained these concepts with research and his own personal experience. This book is a good read and, I believe, will be useful for anyone interested in exploring the topics, as well as those that teach and/or give counsel to others. The "Spiritual Mind" will be a good reference book to include in your own personal library.

Pastor Larry White
Community Impact Church

The Spiritual Mind by Dr. Endiryas Hawaz is a must read for believers looking to develop a deeper faith in Christ. To be truly "transformed by the renewing of our minds", we must first understand how the mind works in conjunction with the Spirit. Dr. Hawaz details this process and truly brings enlightenment to the subject of having the mind of Christ. I highly recommend this for any Christian brave enough to take a deeper journey in the faith.

- Dr. Jamie Jones,
Pastor Trinity Church, Deltona, Fl
Author "The Left-Handed Warrior" and "Kill the Giant".

"Don't be like children [Immature…] in your thinking…but in your mind be Mature [Adults]."

—1 Corinthians 14:20[1]

---

1 AMP

DEDICATION

This book is dedicated with great love and humility to my dear wife, Martha Tadesse, who has been my spouse for the past thirty-two years, and to my beloved children, Pastor Ebenezer, Binyam, Barnabas, and Abigail.

TABLE OF CONTENTS

Prologue

Everyone wants to be successful and have joy in their lives. Do you ever feel like you are carrying around loss, sadness, anger, or other burdens? Do you look inside or outside yourself to fix these feelings? Have you ever considered the God-given power of your mind?

Sometimes the loss, sadness, anger, and feelings of inferiority we feel are not our own but something we carry around from either family or society. Many of our problems are not ours but burdens that others have placed on us since childhood. These burdens have passed from us to the next generation, and they stick. Because of burdens, not only can we pollute the next generation, but we bring this same burden to the church and unwittingly shake off our dirt there too. This becomes readily apparent when it darkens the church, which is supposed to be a light but becomes more of a problem than a solution.

The Beginning of My Life

I was born and raised in Addis Ababa, the capital city of Ethiopia. After accepting the Lord as my personal Savior, I sang in the church where I grew up with young people my age. In my teenage years, I had a dream to travel all over Ethiopia with the song God gave me. Because of this desire, all I thought and meditated about was singing. In those days, I didn't have many responsibilities in life, so I had a lot of free time. Outside of school, I spent most of my time in prayer and reading the Word of God, singing songs, writing poetry, or composing tunes. I used to devote about five to seven hours each day on these thoughts. I was so preoccupied that I couldn't think of anything else.

My life changed when I was singing in the village of Mekanissa; I heard a man giving training about the renewal of the mind and the connection of the soul. Until that time, I had never heard anyone talk on this topic. However, the man said something that stuck with me to this day. He said, "One of the things I care most about in my life and take care of on purpose is my mind."

I don't know why, but this man's words have been my words ever since. I always talk to myself and say that one of the most important things I care about is my mind. Even though I have experienced many difficult times in my life, those problems did not make me lose hope but trained me for the next chapters of my life. When I'm faced with any problem that hurts my feelings, my first thought is to protect my sanity. I immediately take my mind off the thing that has come to hurt me, and I take care of my mind by reading the Word of God and spending time in prayer.

The Power of the Mind

Fear and I have been enemies ever since I knew myself. In no way could I freely share my thoughts in a place where more than one person was present. I never thought that anyone would take my ideas seriously. It had a huge impact on who I wanted to be and what I wanted to do. Even in school, I was afraid to raise my hand in class to answer the questions asked by the teacher.

As soon as I started my preaching service, I had the opportunity to share a word at the Youth for Christ Saturday program at the Geja Word of Life Church (one of the largest denominations in Ethiopia). At that time, I was more into singing and not the sermon. I don't know how it happened, but one day I was destined to preach. An elder of our church looked at me worriedly because it was my first time preaching in the middle of a large congregation. Endiryas said, "Are you afraid?" I said, "Yes, I am very scared." He came close to me, laid his hand on me, prayed a few times, and said, "How do you feel now?" I replied, "I feel worse." I remember that he opened the office door and pushed me into the church where the people were singing.

That day, when I preached, my whole body was trembling. I suffered a lot from this problem, but one day when I was studying my Bible, I read the words in 2 Timothy 1:7[2] that came into me with power as it

---

2 KJV

said, "For God hath not given us the spirit of fear; but of power, and of love, and of a sound mind." The secret of my problem was revealed to me. There is something called the spirit of fear. Until that day, I thought the fear was mine, but then I realized that it wasn't. I realized how much the enemy had held me captive. Since then, the inner potential and gifts that the Lord of my life had placed in me started to be revealed and impact many people.

As the Ethiopian saying goes, "Once a thief is caught, no stick is necessary." From that day forward, I began to oppose the spirit of fear with great fury. Every time I felt a sense of dread, I began to resist, quoting the verse with the knowledge of this word. For many years, I had lived believing that I was a coward in my mind. Therefore, to alter this inner attitude, I used to announce to myself over and over for months, sometimes softly but often loudly, "God hath not given me the spirit of fear, but instead gives me the spirit of power, of love, and of a sound mind."

Today I am able to share my ideas, sing, or preach without fear. Thank God I am completely free from the spirit of fear except to respect God's platform and fear God. Whether it is in my spiritual or physical life, I will never allow the enemy to put any negative thought in my mind or anything that is not according to God's Word. I have learned that by keeping my mind I can keep my life. I realized that if I start allowing the small seed of negative thought to grow even for a few minutes, it will become a big tree and become a trap for me.

I went to Minnesota and served as a pastor for twenty-seven years. I have learned a great lesson during all those years of pastoral service. Apart from the influence of the enemy, the negative influence of their upbringing has prevented many from reaching their goal in life. I see that they are unaware of the influence of negative thinking. Because of this problem, many are prevented from serving God in the way they should. They also are not effective in life.

For this reason, for several years I have tried to research how a person can use and protect the human mind. I have heard many spiritual teachings on this topic repeatedly, so I know that the mind can be used and changed for the glory of God. I spent more than three years writing this book.

I have tried to read various books written on this topic from both the spiritual and scientific worlds. I have studied my Bible, especially the New Testament, from the point of view of the renewal of the mind and only through the lens of this topic. I taught a series of lectures on the same topic for nineteen weeks at the church where I used to serve. I am not a psychiatrist or a psychologist by profession, but I have tried to read the writings of these experts to the best of my ability. It gives me a better understanding of today than yesterday. In my personal life, studying my mind has benefited me immensely.

I know all of this is like scooping water from the ocean of knowledge with a spoon. Although the main purpose of my message is based on biblical teaching, I have tried to make it accessible to everyone by showing the relationship between the ideas of the scientific world and the truth of the spiritual world. I have tried to present my ideas in a simple language that can be understood by everyone. Finally, I have written this book, with the help of God, for the many who are in mental prisons, for those who want to live a successful life, and for all those who want to change themselves in their Christian life and make history by changing our world.

PART ONE

Chapter 1—Human Wholeness

First Thessalonians 5:23,[3] "And the very God of peace sanctify you wholly; and I pray God your whole spirit and soul and body be preserved blameless unto the coming of our Lord Jesus Christ."

The Bible says in Psalm 139:14 that mankind is fearfully and wonderfully made. When the psalmist David was quickened to God's Spirit, he clearly understood this was true of him, so he did not fear. Instead, he acknowledged that he was created wonderfully and fearfully as God had declared. Indeed, there is nothing in God's created world that is not good.

However, man (meant broadly as mankind: male and female) is God's highest creation because we are made in the image and likeness of God Himself. Even Lucifer, a created angelic being who was famous for his beauty before his fall, could not compare in any way with man. Not only was man created by God's wonderful wisdom, but no one and nothing is more loved by God than man.

Understanding Wholeness

What distinguishes man from the other creatures as both wonderful and fearful? First Thessalonians 5:23: this verse identifies the three components of human identity—spirit, soul, and body—and declares the truth that these three make up the whole person.

The word "wholeness" clearly shows that man is not just one thing—not just a body or just a mind, and these three elements are what separates

---

3 KJV

man from other creatures. Genesis 2:7[4] says, "And the Lord God formed man of the dust of the ground, and breathed into his nostrils the breath of life; and man became a living soul." The fact that the human personality consists of two identities, one in the spirit and the other in the body, makes him a unique creation with his soul as the third part.

The Distinction between Humans and Other Creatures

Clearly, God created all things and not just man. However, what makes man different from other creatures is that other creatures do not have spirit, soul, and body. Some have a spirit but are created without a natural body. Others have a natural body and soul but are created without a spirit.

Angels (both evil and holy) are spirits, but they do not have a physical body.

Psalm 104:4 and Hebrews 1:7 tell us God makes His angels spirits. Because of this, angels are incorporeal and have no legal right to enter this world. However, angels can temporarily appear on earth in the form of humans. In Genesis 19:1–3 and Hebrews 13:2, it states that angels are not bound by earthly laws because they do not come in physical body. Because of this, they do not have the right to live on earth, so they come to earth for a while and return to the spirit world after fulfilling their purpose. The only way evil spirits can enter the earth is by seeking an earthly body to live in like that of a human or animal (Matthew 12:43–45). In Matthew 8:28–34, we read they were seen entering both humans and pigs.

Animals have body and soul (breath), but they have no spirit.

Ecclesiastes 3:19–21 tells us that the spirit of human beings goes up and the souls of animals come down to earth. Psalm 32:9[5] says, "Do not be like the horse or the mule, which have no understanding but must be controlled by bit and bridle or they will not come to you." This verse shows us that these animals do not have spiritual understanding. When talking about man, Job 32:8[6] says he makes the distinction plain by stating that he possesses the spirit of discernment,

4 KJV
5 NKJV
6 KJV

"but there is a spirit in man; and the inspiration of the Almighty giveth them understanding."

Lord Jesus Is Perfect Man and Perfect God

In Hebrews 10:5[7] we read, "Therefore, when He came into the world, He said: 'Sacrifice and offering You did not desire, but a body You have prepared for Me,'" speaking about the Lord Jesus. Hebrews 2:14[8] tells us, "Inasmuch then as the children have partaken of flesh and blood, He Himself likewise shared in the same, that through death He might destroy him who had the power of death, that is, the devil." Because of this, while the Lord Jesus was perfect God, when He put on human flesh, He was a perfect man and was called the Son of Man. Before He took on human flesh, He was spirit and had no physical body. This is why the writer of Hebrews spoke of the Lord Jesus as having taken on flesh when He entered the world. God created the natural order, and He designed the world so that the only natural right to enter this world and live is to put on a body. It is not possible to be a living creature on this earth without a body.

God is the Creator and true God of all things. Since God has made the law of creation, He usually does not violate it. He is a God who honors His word, and He made the ordered world to be the way it is so no one can live outside of His natural laws.

Only a human being has his own spirit, soul, and body at the same time. For this reason, only a human has the natural authority to live on earth and has the right to communicate with the spirit world while living on earth. What makes a person human is that the three parts (spirit, soul, and body) are united, and a person can relate in the natural world and in the spiritual world.

Man and His Creation

The book of Genesis divides the creation process into two parts. The first mentions God's creation of everything except man, while the second talks about the creation of Adam and Eve. With His word, God made

---

7 NKJV
8 NKJV

creation out of nothing. When the Bible says He created everything from nothing, the word that's used is taken from Latin (*ex nihilo*) and literally means from nothing. This word shows that before creation, there was nothing and no one before God Himself. When God created the world out of nothing, He showed that the one and only Creator is God Himself.

- "In the beginning God created the heavens and the earth" (Genesis 1:1).[9]

- "All things were made through Him, and without Him was not one thing made" (John 1:3).[10]

- "By the word of the Lord were the heavens made; and all the host of them by the breath of his mouth." In verse 9, "he spake, and it was done; he commanded, and it stood fast" (Psalm 33:6–9).[11]

In Acts 17:24 it says that God created the world and everything in it. Hebrews 11:3 says that the worlds were prepared by the word of God. Therefore, we take by faith that what is seen is not made from what is visible. When God speaks in the Bible about how He did this, Romans 4:17 tells us He called the non-existence by His name and brought it from non-existence to existence. In Psalm 90:2, we learn that before the mountains were born, before the earth and the world were made, "from everlasting to everlasting [He is] God." He is not only talking about His existence before creation but that the creation was made from nothing.

Therefore, if God made creation from nothing, it's easy to see that God is the Creator who existed before all creation and is not a created being. God's unique standing as Creator and His eternal presence before the world began to show us that God is the only God, and He alone deserves to be worshiped. For this reason, man should not worship creation in any way or seek happiness and satisfaction from creation. It is foolish to do so.

God made man from the dust of the ground, preparing his body and breathing His own breath (spirit) into it. Man became an incredible creature of two worlds who comprehends the spiritual world with his

---

9 NIV
10 NKJV
11 KJV

spirit and comprehends the natural world with his body. The natural and spiritual worlds were intertwined.

A person cannot be confused with the world of angels or the world of animals. A man is neither a beast nor an angel. But by God's marvelous creation, man is a lofty and special creation, made to dwell above both animals and angels. He was spiritual in spirit, physical in body, and the three together were named man via the medium of the soul. A man is a nobleman from two realms who lives in both. A man is a nobleman, created in the image and likeness of God, from two realms who can actively engage in both the physical and the spiritual.

The Creation of Adam and Eve

God created the world in three ways. The first has a sense of awareness, the second has self-awareness, and the third has God's awareness and is made to know themselves in a specific way. Only man, as a magnificent creation, is endowed with all three, namely feeling, identity, and knowledge of God. The name Adam means "soil, mud, or clay" because human flesh is generated from dirt.

The three primary terms in human creation are significant and ought to be highlighted.

- God formed him (his body)—Genesis 2:7
- He breathed into his nostrils (his spirit)—Zechariah 12:1
- Man became a soul or a living soul—1 Corinthians 15:45

When he says dust, we recall:

- "Until you return to the ground, for from it you were taken; For you are dust, And to dust you shall return" (Genesis 3:19).12
- "He remembers that we are [merely] dust" (Psalm 103:14).13
- "Then the dust [out of which God made man's body] will return to the earth as it was, and the spirit will return to God who gave it" (Ecclesiastes 12:7).[14]

12 NKJV
13 NKJV
14 NKJV

Although this human man (made from soil) returned to the soil due to sin, God's original aim for man was for Adam and Eve to multiply and fill the world, as indicated in Genesis 1:26, and bring forth a God-fearing generation to govern eternally on God's behalf and to be the embodiment of God's glory and character on earth. This means that the spiritual world would find a body, shelter, or tabernacle (live) on earth without being hindered, and God's great divine plan was implemented on earth without limitation through the human spirit. However, when the human spirit died due to sin, the heavenly world and the natural world were separated by death, and even the body, which was allowed to live on earth for a while, was condemned to return to the soil from which it came.

The Human Spirit

The Bible says that there is a spirit in man. He also calls man a spirit. As the Bible says, "It is flesh born of flesh. It is spirit born of spirit" (John 3:6). He says that our flesh is flesh because we were born from earthly parents. No matter how we look at it, the source of the human spirit is God and not the earth.

As the human spirit is given by God, Isaiah 42:5 describes it as "who gives breath to the people on it, And spirit to those who walk on it."[15] In Zechariah 12:1 it says that it is God who "formed the spirit of man within him."[16]

There is no doubt that man is flesh. God told Adam from the beginning in Genesis 3 that "you are dust and to dust you will return."[17] When He says you are dust, He doesn't mean you are not valuable to God. It is to identify the essence of the body and say that the source is the soil. It proves that it is impossible to deny that man has a physical identity since our identity is our source.

On the other hand, in the New Testament, John says that he is born of the flesh, not that he has flesh, but that he is flesh. In the same way, he who is born of the Spirit is said to be of the Spirit, but he does not say that he has a Spirit. Because the origin of the human spirit itself is from

---

15 NKJV
16 NKJV
17 Genesis 3:19 (AMP)

the breath of God, man is not a changeable instinct that becomes flesh when he wants it or spirit when he wants it. Man is God's masterpiece that is both spirit and flesh at the same time.

To correct one false teaching does not give us the right to violate another truth. The Bible puts it in a balanced way. Man is both flesh and spirit at the same time. My body is my physical self given to live on earth; my spirit is my spiritual self given to live in the spirit world.

Understanding the Difference

The difference lies in understanding the purpose for which both are given. Body and spirit are separate in their creation and the purpose for which they were created. The ability of the spirit is much different from the body.

The flesh is limited in many things. But the spirit is much more independent than the body. We can only be physically present in one place at a time, but the spirit is far and wide. Those who live according to the flesh will never be able to understand the things of the spirit, and they cannot please God in any way (Romans 8:8). But spiritual people examine everything. "But the natural man receiveth not the things of the Spirit of God: for they are foolishness unto him: neither can he know them, because they are spiritually discerned" (1 Corinthians 2:14).[18]

Man is flesh, and man is spirit. However, the spirit is far superior to the body. Although the human spirit is not visible to the physical eye, it is the main essence of who we are. I believe the Bible teaches that when God created us from the beginning, knowing God's will and purpose in the spiritual world through our spirit, we were called to live in the execution of that will in our body on earth.

Except for the first humans, Adam and Eve, it was birth that made man spirit and flesh (John 3:5). What gives man a natural identity is that he is born from his natural parents, and what makes him spiritual is that he is born from the word and Spirit of God.

Some teachers teach that the body is only a residence, but this is only half of the idea. Indeed, the human spirit resides in the human body.

---

18 KJV

This means that the human body is not only the home of the human spirit. The human body is not only a dwelling place for the spirit but also its identity as long as it is on earth. A human being is both a spirit and a body at the same time and is governed by the medium of the soul. In their teachings, some teachers say that the body is the dwelling place of the human spirit and has no identity. I say that this part should be corrected because the body is not only the residence of the human spirit. Without a human body, the human spirit cannot live on earth.

Although the Bible refers to the human body as a shelter, it is more than that. In 2 Corinthians 4:16[19] it says, "For which cause we faint not; but though our outward man perishes, yet the inward man is renewed day by day." He called man his spirit inward and his body outward. Both are called man; one, the inward man; the other, outward man. The difference is that we can see the outward man but cannot see the inward man with our physical eyes.

Just as the human spirit has wishes and desires, so does the human flesh. The need for both depends on the type of their nature. Flesh from dust and spirit from spirit. While the flesh seeks earthly things, the spirit seeks spiritual things. For this reason, since they both have identity, in Galatians 5:17[20] it says, "For the flesh lusts against the Spirit, and the Spirit against the flesh; and these are contrary to one another, so that you do not do the things that you wish." This verse shows clearly that there is a war of interests. Because both are our identity, as much as the inward man (our spirit) has a desire, the outward man (our flesh) also has a desire. Although the battlefield is our mind, the desire is both physical and spiritual according to their need. The soul is the medium between the two and is the judge.

All of us who live as human beings know how much the flesh has the potential to rise against the desire of the spirit and how much the desire of the spirit has a strong antagonism to the flesh. If it hadn't been for the flesh, Paul would not have stated, "I discipline my body and bring it into submission" (1 Corinthians 9:27).[21] It is for this reason that in the book of Romans Paul said not to fulfill the desires of the flesh. We might

19 KJV
20 NKJV
21 NKJV

conclude from all of this that the body is not only just the garment of the spirit but also the outward identity of man. In fact, in John 6:63, the Lord Jesus said that the flesh is good for nothing; however, the context of the passage shows that since the Lord spoke about spiritual life, His true meaning is that flesh and blood will not inherit the kingdom of God, so the flesh we wear will be of no use to the world to come. This is because our body is corrupted by sin.

Our body is the most important and most valuable part of us to live on this earth. If this was not the case, how could it have been written to honor God in your body? Our body does not understand spiritual things. For this reason, when we want to live the spiritual life, flesh will not obey. However, it should not be forgotten that when the flesh submits to the spirit, it also greatly contributes to God's work and service. If it were not so, the Lord Jesus would not have had to take on flesh. If there was no body, where would the spirit stay? How was the spirit manifested on earth? If the flesh was not the outward identity of man, how could it fight against the spirit? Clothes cannot be an identity, so they would not have the ability to fight.

God honored and glorified the Lord Jesus because He committed Himself to God through numerous prayers and supplications so that the pain that befell His body throughout the months of His flesh would not damage His spirituality. As a result, He reestablished man's dominion over the natural world. This is why it should be our daily job to make our body a tremendous instrument to honor and exalt the Lord by surrendering our body to God's glory and making it a tool for our Lord's purpose and will. As we see in Romans 12:1–2, our greatest service and worship is to offer this body as a holy and living sacrifice to God every day. As I have stated above, when the spirit is the ruler of the body and the body lives for the glory of God, we call that the Christian life of victory. But when the flesh rules over the spirit, a person lives only for the flesh; we call that a carnal Christian life.

Our body is the instrument that gives us the right to exist in the natural world. It is our only tool to express the spiritual world in the natural world. But if this flesh is satisfied without limits and dominates the spirit, it destroys the meaning of living. We should make sure that our flesh lives under the control of our spirit. Only a believer who fulfills God's will in the spiritual world by controlling the flesh can be successful on earth and glorify God.

Man is both flesh and spirit at the same time. But the essence of the body was given to be a servant of God's will for the spirit who excels in all things. When the flesh obeys the spirit, life is sweet, but when the flesh is subordinated to the spirit, life loses its flavor. It would be like putting the cart before the horse, for the cart was made for the horse. For this reason, as long as we live on earth, our major homework is to subjugate our physical identity to spiritual identity and live as a reason for God's will that is in heaven to be fulfilled on earth.

Apart from this, the attitude that only focuses on the spirit or the body is what makes us a tool for Satan, for both are who we are. If we see a person only in terms of his body, he will be alien to the world of the spirit. If we say that the flesh is of no use and only the spirit is the main thing, it is opening the way for flesh to be satiated. But when we make both take their place and serve God with who they are, we can live a right and balanced life. Being both flesh and spirit at the same time is the thing that separates humans from other creatures.

The great false teaching that Satan used after Jesus Christ's ascension to oppose his great saving work was by saying that Jesus did not come in the flesh. This was one of the major false teachings that the apostles fought against. If we say that Christ did not appear in the flesh, it is because it undermines the Christian faith. If He had not taken on flesh, He would not have been able to represent us. That is why He is said to be like His brothers. He did not contain the seed of angels, but He took on Him the seed of Abraham. Christ putting on flesh as a man is one of the most important teachings of Christianity.

When the Bible discusses the human spirit's relationship with God, God is referred to as the God of the human spirit. He also refers to Him as His Father. His deity is for everyone, and His fatherhood is for everyone who believes in Christ Jesus and is saved (Numbers 16:22). When the Bible declares that He is the God of the spirits of all flesh, He is not only the God of all spirit of flesh but also the Father of the spirit of believers

(Hebrews 12:9). This is why it is said that they were born of God and not of flesh and blood or the will of man (John 1:13).

The main purpose of this book is to highlight the work and responsibility of the soul, which can connect the spirit and the body in order to fulfill the will of God and use His will to highlight His responsibility on earth. One of our greatest rewards before the Lord is when we surrender our bodies as living and holy sacrifices daily so that we can know and live according to His will. This can happen only if we know God's will through our spirit, which is God's lamp, by renewing our mind and subjecting our body to live according to His will and to fulfill His purpose.

Chapter 2—The Soul of Man

Matthew 22:37,[22] "Jesus replied: 'Love the Lord your God with all your heart and with all your soul and with all your mind.'"

The first mention of the word "soul" in the Bible is in Genesis 2:7. After human flesh was formed from the dust of the earth, when God breathed into his nostrils, man became a living soul. The word soul in Greek is *psyche*, and in Hebrew *nephesh*; we find it mentioned many times in the Old and New Testaments. Most often, the definition is "a living creature or a breathing creature." Man is a living, moving, and soulful creature.

If we look at Genesis 2:7, it says that man's body is made from the dust of the earth and his spirit from the breath of God, but it does not mention the soul from which it is made. Where did the human soul come from? What is the location? It says that when the breath of God entered the earthly body of man, immediately man became a living soul. We can assume that the word "became" is a result of the interaction between the spirit and the flesh.

The presence of the soul is an event not from the earth or from the breath of God. The soul is derived from the body and spirit. Based on this, we can think that the soul is the result of the relationship between the body and the spirit. When I say the soul was found, I don't mean that this is a coincidence. For the soul is created by God's wisdom and wonderful ability. But we can see that its creation is not from the soul or body from the breath of God but from the presence of the relationship between the two. Of course, the soul is different from the body and spirit. Although the human soul is not a spirit, it has a significant contact with the spirit world. In the same way, the soul is not a body but has a clear connection with the natural world.

---

22 NIV

According to this theory, we can see that the human soul has a relationship with both worlds. If the breath of God did not exist in the earthly body of man, what would the soul rest in? Or how would a person have a living soul if his earthly body did not receive the breath of God? But when the spirit and body meet, the soul acts as a mediator between the two recognizing both the natural and the spiritual worlds of the human being.

When is the human soul created when we are born? Although scientists have debated different theories on this question, some say that the minute the male and female seeds meet, the human soul begins within us. When they say that the plan of human life is created at that moment, they say that after that, just like an engineer builds a building following the plan of the building, our body and body cells follow that and shape the child's physical identity. On the other hand, some people are teaching that the soul and the spirit are one. But this is not a biblical view at all. A soul is not a spirit. A spirit is not a soul. In many ways, the Bible says that there is a difference between soul and spirit. Hebrews 4:12[23] says, "The word of God…piercing even to the division of soul and spirit, and of joints and marrow." Apostle Paul said in 1 Thessalonians 5:23,[24] "May God himself, the God of peace, sanctify you through and through. May your whole spirit, soul and body be kept blameless at the coming of our Lord Jesus Christ." He showed that the whole of man is made of three things and that holiness is needed in all three things. Although in some parts of the Bible it is difficult to distinguish between them, the soul and spirit are presented interchangeably, but there is a difference between them.

The Bible says that human physical life is in the blood like any other animal. For the life of the flesh is the blood. But man has a spiritual life because he also has a spirit. This spiritual life is not derived from the blood of the physical body. Rather, since the source of human spiritual life is the breath of God, it is possible to live without the body. Because the life of the spirit is the Spirit of God, it is eternal and indestructible. But when the spirit of Man is separated from the Spirit of God, the human spirit becomes dead. This is called spiritual death. When God said to Adam that he would die, we know that he did not die in his body first,

---

23 NKJV
24 NIV

but rather that he lived for 900 years. How can we say that he is dead? It is because he cannot have spiritual life apart from God.

Death means separation. According to this interpretation, the Bible calls the separation of the soul from the body physical death, while the separation of the spirit from God is called spirit death or spiritual death. When the Lord Jesus stated, "Let the dead bury their own dead" (Matthew 8:22),[25] He was referring to the two kinds of death. He meant people who died in their spirit when He said "the dead," and He meant a person whose soul had departed from his body when He said "their own dead." He was discussing both deaths claiming that the person who died in spirit went to bury the one who died in body.

We see the word "soul" also used for animals. In Genesis 1:21 He called the living creatures that move in the water. In Genesis 1:24 and 1:30, He says the same thing about the souls of the birds of the air and the animals of the earth. The word "creatures" is mentioned in the King James Version, which is translated as "soul" in Hebrew. However, the human soul is much more unique than the animal soul.

The human soul has knowledge, morality, and will. And because the human soul has the will, it is able to make a mistake. Because of this, he sinned and was lost, so he needed a savior. But animals are not like that. Their knowledge is very limited and instinctive. Because they have no morals, they have no laws to break. Because of this they do not sin; they do not need a savior because they do not perish if they do not sin. But man has the ability to choose, reason, and see tomorrow and live today with his knowledge and will. But animal knowledge is instinctive and only helps to move and keep them alive. Since the human soul is related to the spirit, their difference is as distant as heaven and earth. For animals have no spirit. This is one of the highlights of human dignity (http://www.newdualism.org/papers/R.Scott/Scott-PSCF6-2012.pdf).

Three Parts of the Soul

The soul is the medium in the human being. If man didn't have a soul, he wouldn't be able to know or realize his spiritual and natural identity. We know about our body and spirit through our soul. The spiritual part

---

25 NIV

of the human soul is called the mind, and the natural part is called the brain or head. The soul is the part of us where knowledge, emotion, and will are found. The human soul is the part that is immortal like the spirit and can live forever apart from the body. The Lord Jesus spoke about the immortality of the soul, "Do not fear those who kill the body but cannot kill the soul."[26] He showed the immortality of the soul in Matthew 10:28[27] by saying, "Fear the one who can destroy both soul and body in hell." The soul has three parts within it. Knowledge, emotion, and will. We find these three prominently placed in the Word of God.

- Knowledge

Proverbs 2:10[28] says, "When wisdom enters your heart, And knowledge is pleasant to your soul." Knowledge makes the soul happy because knowledge is in the soul. Proverbs 24:13–14[29] continues with, "My son, eat honey because *it is* good, and the honeycomb *which is* sweet to your taste; So *shall* the knowledge of wisdom *be* to your soul." Wisdom and knowledge are related to the soul because the soul's ability to experience knowledge is in wisdom. Knowledge and wisdom are in the mind.

Psalm 139:14 states, "I will praise You, for I am fearfully and wonderfully made; Marvelous are Your works, And that my soul knows very well."[30] The psalmist relates the knowledge of God's wonderful works to his soul because knowledge resides in the soul. Because knowledge is absorbed by the soul, our soul is filled with knowledge. Since knowledge is in the mind, it cannot be questioned that our mind is in our soul. And it is not good for the soul to be without knowledge.

- Emotion

Emotions include likes, hates, happiness, sadness, and so forth. Song of Solomon 1:7[31] says, "Tell me, you whom my soul loves." "My soul loves you" is significant evidence that the emotion is in the soul. We see in

---

26 Matthew 10:28 (NKJV)
27 NKJV
28 NKJV
29 NKJV
30 NKJV
31 AMP

Isaiah 61:10,[32] "I will greatly rejoice in the Lord, My soul shall be joyful in my God." Happiness is in the soul, and my soul rejoices in my God. In Psalm 86:4,[33] the psalmist sings, "Rejoice the soul of Your servant, for to You, O Lord, I lift up my soul."

- Will

There is a will in the soul. In Job 6:7[34], "My soul refuses to touch them; Such things are like loathsome food to me [sickening and repugnant]." The Amplified Bible translation translates "my body" as "my soul refuses to touch them." In Numbers 30:2,[35] "If a man makes a vow to the Lord, or swears an oath to bind himself by some agreement, he shall not break his word." The phrase "binds himself with an oath" means he binds his soul. This word is mentioned eleven times in this chapter; the main notion is "to decide." The soul is a source of knowledge, information, emotion, and consent. We know by our soul. What we love and what we hate is in our soul. We see right and left and decide based on our knowledge and listen to our emotion.

Soul, Mind, and Brain

Mind is the part of us where human thought, memory, dreaming, and consciousness are located. Mind resides in the soul. There is a good example of the relationship and difference between the mind and the soul, and that is the ocean. We can see the mind as a wave in the ocean. When we see the movement of water on the ocean, we call it a wave or tsunami. But what is called tsunami is the same water on the ocean. It is the same ocean of water that has been moved but given another name.

In the same way, the soul is like the ocean, and the mind is like the wave. If there is movement in the human soul, it is the mind that moves. Since the mind is in the soul, we can think of it as the soul that moved. The mind is a part of the soul. It is a movement of the soul because it is a movement of the mind in the soul.

---

32 KJV
33 NKJV
34 AMP
35 NKJV

The head or brain is the physical part of the soul. The physical part of the human brain works in unison with the non-physical soul. For example, just like a computer has hardware and software and one does not benefit from the other, the two parts work together. In the same way, the thoughts we think are related to the brain and can stimulate emotions by triggering various hormones. This is why when we feel happy or sad in our mind, smiles and laughter or crying and sadness are prominently displayed on our body.

Mental Illness

Our brain is the natural part of our mind, so like any other part of our body, it is susceptible to disease, injury, and danger. It can also be cured by treatment. It is often seen that many people are confused by some of the symptoms that Christians show when they are experiencing dementia, depression, or various other mental illnesses. A Christian may lose his intelligence or memory due to an accident or illness. It is known that there are conditions in which his health can improve if he is treated at this time.

We should not be surprised if a believer goes through some mental problems. He may feel suicidal due to anxiety, fear, or other reasons. Any part of our body can get sick, and our brain is one of the parts of our body. Moreover, unless he receives treatment, anyone can kill himself. But I don't think this person would lose his salvation because what he did was something he wouldn't have done if he had a healthy brain. Everything he did was motivated by illness, not because he intentionally ignored the Word of God or because of denial. A rational believer would never be able to destroy himself without a good reason. I believe individuals can reach this conclusion because of one of four reasons: first, when the brain, like any other organ, becomes ill and is unable to think effectively; second, when he is unable to use his thoughts effectively as a result of an injury; third, when he changes his mind about sad or frightening occurrences in life and cannot be consoled and troubles his mind with negative thoughts more than he should and develops depression and loses control of his mind; and fourth, when possessed and substantially affected by an enemy demon.

The devil, our adversary, does not simply influence the thoughts of unbelievers; he will fight a fierce struggle against those who live as believers. In my opinion, what he does to our minds is more difficult than any enemy attack. The major reason for this is that if the devil obtains control of our minds, he also gains control of our world. Our thoughts are under the sway of bad spirits just as much as our spirits and bodies. Satan cannot possess a Christian, yet he may dominate his thoughts if the believer is not careful. When the mind is occupied, everything else is occupied as well. If a believer is unable to control his thoughts, Satan can take away his ability to reason and decide, putting him in danger of harming himself and others. Because of this, ministers and doctors both make mistakes. Believers make everything spiritual and pray for the person in need of treatment as from an evil spirit without distinguishing the root of the problem, and doctors try to help the person possessed by the evil spirit with treatment.

Mental illness can be spiritual or physical. If it is spiritual, a spiritual solution is needed, and if it is physical, it needs to be solved medically. If people in the medical world are not believers, they cannot understand the spiritual world, so if they do not take the demon-possessed person to church and have the spirit come out, all their efforts in medicine are in vain. Christians consider all mental problems to be from the spirit, and it is better to help the patient with healing gifts or go to doctors for help.

Brain and Mind

Our brain is not eternal, so it can die with the rest of our body. But since our mind is eternal, it will live forever even apart from our body. This is why we can understand and think without our brain after death. The brain is made up of nerve cells and blood vessels. The mind is the thinking and information-gathering part of the human. The brain is the physical home of the mind, which is the electric impulses that move the thought or power the generator or move the device.

The human mind is not inanimate but is related to the human body, and the two together constitute the individual identity of the human being. The brain is the main nervous system, and its primary function is to receive, organize, and distribute information. It is also the control center of the body. This is the part that helps us to understand our thoughts, feelings, and environment. But the mind is the manifestation of thoughts, emotions, dreaming, and memory, and it is the part of us that controls knowledge and identifies why we do what we do.

The soul of man should live in the body but should not be limited to the body. Our body can only be in one place at a time, but the soul can explore yesterday, today, and tomorrow by dreaming with thoughts outside of our body. Apart from that, when mental activity is healthy and experienced, man has a great ability to believe that unexpected and unprecedented things will happen. For that reason, he works his body with his thoughts, changes the shape, size, and natural characteristics of new things, and has a great ability to create great discoveries with his creativity.

We have no problem moving and using our body parts. The reason for this is that it is easy to move our body parts because they are seen by our physical eyes, and when we touch them, we understand them in a way that is related to our feelings. But since we cannot see our soul with our eyes and touch it with our body parts, we often find it difficult to use our minds properly. The soul is not visible to the eye, but we use it every day even if we don't notice it. No one lives without thinking, without happiness or sadness, and without making big or small decisions every day.

The problem is that we are not able to filter the knowledge that we put into our mind deliberately, or we do not properly use the emotions that we feel. This is why we don't use the content and quality of the decisions we make every day as we want and in the right way. It is for this reason that many people's lives fall into harm's way, and they leave this world without using the inner skills they have been given during their lifetime. Above all, many Christians do not know that the contribution of their soul is very high after they are saved. Without spiritual knowledge, they will be influenced, whether it is a person, a situation, or an evil spirit, to not live a life of victory that glorifies God.

My hopes and supplications are that after you complete reading this book, you will comprehend the purpose of living on this earth for the rest of your days, utilizing your mind to live for the glory of God and using your inner powers to live overflowing life for yourself, the church, and the entire world.

Chapter 3—Human Identity and Mind

Romans 8:5–6,[36] "For those who live according to the flesh set their minds on the things of the flesh, but those who live according to the Spirit, the things of the Spirit. For to be Carnally minded is death, but to be spiritually minded is life and peace."

Man is a creature with a soul that lives between his spirit and his body. This soul has a mind. There are two types of human mind. The main reason for this is that the Bible presents the human mind in two ways. He calls one the spiritual mind and the other the carnal mind. We have one mind that performs two functions. We use our minds for both.

As we see in Romans 8:5, the carnal mind and the spiritual mind made man to have two forms. A person cannot think about both his body and his spirit at the same time, but he can go from one to the other in an instant. When he wants the spiritual and when he wants the natural, he has the ability to think one time of righteousness and another time of sin. When we think of the things of the flesh, we are using the carnal mind; when we think about spiritual things, we are using the spiritual mind.

As Galatians 5:17 says, the battle is always between the flesh and the spirit, but the battlefield is our mind. This war is clearly known to all of us until it seems that there are two people inside us. But the winner of the battle will be known only after the decision. Any of our actions are defined after a decision. God gave the will to mankind. This made him choose what he wanted and live as he wanted. This is why Galatians 5:17 says you cannot do what you want. The words "you want" mean "what you desire."

The reason for this is that both flesh and spirit have interests. To choose what we want, we must be spiritual or carnal because we cannot be and

---

36 NKJV

do both at the same time. Although man can choose and live between the natural and spiritual worlds, he cannot choose and live in both at the same time. He chooses one and discards the other. When he decides on one, he leaves the other. No matter which one he chooses, the decision will be either good or bad, spiritual or physical.

Anyone should be aware of these two minds and how to utilize them properly, especially those who have accepted Christ as their Savior. In addition to failing to understand the meaning of life, he spends his time always questioning, confused, and living an unsuccessful life. Above all, he won't be able to be ready for the heavenly and everlasting kingdom, which is the major reason we're here on earth. This would be a huge loss.

Mind in the Sight of God's Word

In Hebrews 4:12[37] it says, "For the word of God *is* living and powerful, and sharper than any two-edged sword, piercing even to the division of soul and spirit, and of joints and marrow, and is a discerner of the thoughts and intents of the heart." Man is a noble creation who has been entrusted with great authority and identity so that he can rule the natural world from the spirit world. On the contrary, after we are reborn in Christ Jesus, our capacity and ability to carry out God's thoughts and purposes in the natural world is high.

What is in the spiritual world cannot pass directly from the spirit to the flesh so that God's riches, purposes, and ideas can be expressed in the natural world. The human mind is the way for all spiritual things to pass into the natural world. If we see the human spirit as God's storehouse, God stores all his thoughts, blessings, gifts, and knowledge only in the human spirit. For the spirit of man is the lamp of God.

The human mind is the manager of all spiritual things that God has placed in the human spirit. A manager's main job is to know what is available and make sure that everything is used properly. The human mind is the medium and interface between the body and the spirit because its main task is to manage. But the human body is the servant of the spirit and is the only way for everything in the spiritual and the world of thought to manifest into the natural world.

---

37 NKJV

Every blessing and gift given in the spirit is seen and expressed in the body or the human being. And the flesh cannot do anything on its own without the command of the human mind. Although everything that happens to the human body has a great effect on the soul and spirit, the human body can do nothing without the human mind. This means that as long as the health of our body is not disturbed, everything that happens is only what we think and allow in our mind.

As long as mankind exists on earth, the spirit, soul, and body can never exist without each other. For this reason, it is extremely important to consider that what happens to one can affect all three. To isolate one from the other or to think that one has no influence on the other is foolish and will inevitably lead to danger.

Ignorance of the creation and functioning of the human mind is like blocking the transmission pipeline that is about to be revealed from the spiritual world to the earth. As a person has a holistic identity, it is difficult to say that he has lived a life on this earth until he knows all his identity and uses it properly. Most people are limited by their apparent self, that is, their knowledge of their natural self. When he is hungry, he eats; when he is thirsty, he drinks; when he is tired, he sleeps; he does not find it difficult to rest. But he does not have the right knowledge that his inner self needs food and that he can be tired and strong.

As I tried to mention above, man is not just flesh; he has spirit and soul. Knowing about the mind and understanding how to use the mind is extremely important in order to use it to its fullest potential. Ignoring this and living life only from the point of view of the physical world makes life boring, tiring, and meaningless.

A man has a mind, but he is not a mind. Our minds, like any other component of our body, are a gift from God. Just as we don't lift our hands to walk and move on our feet, the mind is a wonderful inner gift that allows us to think, reason, plan, and dream. Recognizing that our mind is ours, we must utilize it intentionally. The life of a man who does not employ his thoughts is said to be no better than that of an animal. Because it is said that "a man who is in honor, yet does not understand, is like the beasts that perish" (Psalm 49:20).[38] If not utilizing the mind

---

38 NKJV

or having no mind makes a person equivalent to an animal, then using our minds is one of the things that distinguishes us from animals and makes us human.

One of the most severe punishments that God can enforce on a man is to take away his mind, and when he blesses him, he helps him to use his mind. When asked what he wished God to accomplish for Solomon as king, Solomon replied, "Give me the wisdom and understanding to serve before this great nation." He asked for wisdom to use his mind properly instead of what he wanted to do with his physical need. This pleased God. Because of this, He gave him wisdom and understanding as if no one would rise before him or after him. For this is a great blessing. When the Bible talks about Solomon's mind, God expands his heart (mind) like the sand of the sea. For the mind can expand and shrink.

What pleased God was not that Solomon did not ask for the lives of his enemies or his wealth and prosperity with honor, but what pleased Him was that he said that the power of governing a large nation given by God required wisdom. Wisdom is the tool by which we know how to turn knowledge into action. Wisdom is the ability to see earthly problems from a heavenly perspective. Wisdom is the ability to see the problem and the solution with God's eyes. This wisdom is the ability to know which way to direct the mind when considering the natural with the spiritual.

This is the mind that made the state of Israel rich. It is this mind that makes gold as abundant as copper. It is this mind that made it possible to build the temple according to God's command. According to Solomon, it will cause God to bless us without limitations if our mind manages the blessings we are given with wisdom and understanding.

On the other hand, when Nebuchadnezzar finished building Babylon, he said, "Is not this great Babylon that I have built for the house of the kingdom by the might of my power, and for the honor of my majesty?" (Daniel 4:30).[39] Before he could finish his confession, God's judgment came upon him. This great judgment was the taking of his mind. As soon as his mind was taken away, he ate grass like an animal. When seven years passed, God showed that He was thinking about this man. Nebuchadnezzar himself said, "My mind returned to me, and my counselors sought

---

39 KJV

me out." It was their mind that caused Nebuchadnezzar to lose what he had, which caused Solomon to gain what he did not have. When a man is right in his mind, he will start to get what he doesn't have, and what he already has will multiply. When a person is not in the right mind, he loses what he has or lives a meaningless and purposeless animal life.

God's Judgment and Human Mind

In the book of Romans, we see that when God makes judgments, He ruins their minds and gives them over to vanity or to do useless things. When a person loses his mind, he changes the natural use into that which is against nature; then he starts to live without dignity. Romans 1:26,[40] "For even their women did change the natural use into that which is against nature."

These people willingly left God's truth. As much as they refused to honor the Lord, it was their thinking that changed first. When they decided to go with the futility of their thoughts, it was at this point when they became vain in their minds. The NIV translation says in Romans 1:21 that "their thinking became futile and their foolish hearts were darkened." In this section, the word "futile" means that it has no value or use, or it is useless or unable to achieve the desired result, and the word "dark" in this section refers to the absence of exact illumination necessary to know and discern right from evil, respectively.

When man starts thinking of useless thoughts, the mental image is damaged, or the value and weight they give to life is destroyed. At this time their hearts were darkened. Their conscience failed to see and think anything good. Because of this, being alive to evil, their conscience was darkened for good. According to the American Standard Version, "they became vain in their reasonings, and their senseless heart was darkened."

When they are just like this, Romans 1:24 says that God gave them over to the lust of their hearts to the thoughts of impurity. This forced them to humiliate their flesh. Because of this, when their choice is corrupted, or they decide to go with their thoughts in vain, God leaves this mind and gives them over to their own minds and thoughts to think about evil and meaningless things.

---

40 KJV

Romans 1:26[41] closes by saying that "God gave them over to shameful lusts." This is a very important idea because it was when they decided and allowed themselves to turn away from God's truth and knowledge that made them give in to evil thoughts. Romans 1:28[42] states, "Just as they did not think it worthwhile to retain the knowledge of God, so God gave them over to a depraved mind, so that they do what ought not to be done." As I tried to say above, it is inevitable that a thought in our mind will always have an effect on our body. When our thoughts are corrupted, our physical life is corrupted. Our body is the servant of our spirit and the reflection of our thoughts.

To lead a pure life, everyone should only think of pure thought. If he fails to accomplish this, his wicked thoughts continuously undermine his positive views about life and its purpose. This is against God's rule, and as a result, he loses his vision or desire for good things. And God will enable him to act in such a way by giving him up to wicked thoughts first. He is compelled by this to turn to bad and foolish deeds.

God's Knowledge and Human Mind

Knowing what God has prevented these people from reaching in life will help us know what to do so that we do not succumb to this mind. God's great blessing to man is to share and show his thoughts by stating the truth so that the human mind does not go as it likes. This truth is referred to as the knowledge of God according to Romans.

When a person's mind is not filled with God's knowledge, or when he underestimates God's knowledge or fails to emphasize its importance, he gives his mind to another useless knowledge. The word "gave" does not mean that God gave them an evil mind, but it means that He stopped giving or revealing the truth that frees and protects the mind.

One of God's greatest punishments is to give a person over to himself or to an absurd thought. In this section, he says that he revealed the truth to them so that they could know and thank God for everything that should be known. However, whenever you refuse to accept this truth and thank God, God stops sharing His own holy and true thoughts and

---

41 NIV
42 NIV

knowledge so that people will give over to worthless and useless minds. This means that they are given over to any unreal and unholy thoughts and feelings. Mind can never exist without thought or knowledge. He chooses one or the other—the holy or the profane.

One of the ways in which God separated man from animals was to give man the knowledge of God in which to live and to reveal truths. Man is created to live with a balance of conscience so that he can reason and choose the right thing. However, in this place, when man refuses to accept this knowledge, he despises the moral and spiritual knowledge that makes him a great man; instead, he commits himself to living a senseless and unbalanced life where he is not allowed to be or do anything. When he says that he does not accept the truth of God, who made him special and better than all creatures, his thoughts control his personality and make him feel insensitive to do everything that he should not do, and he is forced to live a life no better than an animal.

Romans 1:26–27 addresses that since godless and wicked people, who despised the truth of God, instead of doing what was right for them, began to do what was not right for them. Other translations say that they do "unnatural things." To live according to the purpose and dignity for which man was created, a person must fill his mind with God's knowledge and truth, and he must submit himself to this knowledge and live in that truth.

But when he rejects this knowledge, he gains the power to do what is shameful without shame. This causes them to receive punishment from God. The biggest penalty for humans is their lack of moral integrity, which allows them to live with a loose outlook on life or an unrestrained mind to engage in improper behavior. One of the curses mentioned in Deuteronomy 28:28[43] is that "God will strike you with madness." Human success and happiness lie in living in God's knowledge and truth. Otherwise, instead of sharing God's blessings, man will be forced to live without his mind under the curse of madness.

Being a Christian, I think about what a blessing it is to be able to know and learn the Word of God. What makes a person honorable and makes his life full of honor is his ability to accept any knowledge and truth

43 NKJV

that God reveals to him and to live in that truth. What a wonderful gift! The Word of God, which we read every morning and night, the Word of God, which we learn every Sunday and every conference; how wonderful it is that the Word of God enables us to live a quality life and do the right thing with the right mind, not only by distinguishing between human and animal life but also between humans.

Because the Word feeds our mind with God's knowledge, this word of truth from God controls our emotions and makes us live the holy and quality life we deserve. A person who is filled with God's knowledge and truth from God's Word every day can control his mind and has the ability to distinguish and choose between what is right and what is not and to make the right decision.

Worship and the Human Mind

Without God's truth and knowledge, man cannot offer true worship and serve God properly. A person who despises the truth and knowledge of God, apart from being unable to worship God, gives up worshiping and serving the creature. Since it is one of the main reasons for man's creation, it is impossible to live without worship. Worship is inevitable. Either God or something else. If not the Creator, it is a must to worship the created.

The question is, to whom have we given our minds? A mind devoted to the knowledge of God worships God, but one who despises this great knowledge is forced to worship anything because his choice is to worship something else. True worship is not based on emotion. The source is to receive the true knowledge that God wants to reveal to us through revelation. Worship requires correct knowledge. Worship without knowledge is impossible. When Lord Jesus said to the Samaritan woman that we worship what we know, it was to show that worship is not possible without knowledge and that ignorance changes the direction of worship.

In Romans 1:25, he explained the reason why man gives to himself, "Because they changed the truth of God with a lie and worshiped and served what was created instead of the Creator." Knowing or not knowing God's truth changes the content and form of our worship. Indeed, since God is a spirit, He is worshiped in spirit and in truth. However, it is very important that the mind is filled with the truth and knowledge of God because it is necessary to be right in the mind to worship in the spirit. In Deuteronomy 6:5[44] it states, "You shall love the Lord your God with all your heart, with all your soul, and with all your strength." Those who have lost their minds or do not have proper knowledge of God can never love or worship Him.

Second Corinthians 10:5[45] states, "Casting down arguments and every high thing that exalts itself against the knowledge of God, bringing every thought into captivity to the obedience of Christ." If man's thoughts exalt themselves against the knowledge of God, how can his spirit worship God with a mind against the knowledge of God? True worship comes out of rest, not out of war. I think this is why true worship is largely lost today. If many people start worshiping God without subjecting their minds to the knowledge of God, it is certain that this mind, which has been diluted and corrupted by other knowledge, will not allow them to worship God properly in any way.

God's Knowledge and Truth at the Beginning of Creation

The greatest thing that God gave to Adam was to accept God's knowledge and live foolishly. When he lived in obedience to God in the garden of Eden, everything was subject to him. But when man tried to change God's knowledge with his own knowledge, he ate of the tree. Man knew good and evil. In other words, the man who used to live only in the knowledge of God now chose to use his own rational thinking, thus separating himself from the life of God; the two cannot coexist. One must either accept God's truth and live foolishly or live apart from God's truth with one's own rational knowledge. The problem is that you can't do both at the same time. If we choose rational knowledge of self, then we must live life without God. This makes everything that belongs to God our enemy. Creation is ruled by God's knowledge and thoughts.

Adam had the authority to rule creation only as long as he was willing to live in God's mind. Their departure from God's plan means leaving the authority of the creation that rules according to God's plan. This is why the ground grows thorns and thistles. This is why the beasts and animals

44 NKJV
45 NKJV

stopped being subservient to humans. This is why the thing that was given to man to submit rebelled against man. Not only rebelled, but his life was bitter, sorrowful, sick, and painful and eventually led to death.

Human life begins with the mind and the thoughts and mentalities in the mind. For just as a man thinks, so is he. The first and foremost thing that God asks of us is, "My son, give me your heart" (Proverbs 23:26).[46] Proverbs 4:23[47] states that "for out of it are the issues of life." What a person becomes in life is determined by what they focus on in their heart or mind. What we focus on in mind, one way or the other, will inevitably come out of us.

The apostle Paul's biggest fear about the Corinthians was that Satan would corrupt their thoughts. He knows that if one's thoughts change, one's life will change. When the knowledge of God came to them through the truth of the gospel, it changed their minds and made them sincere and pure. But now, Satan came to destroy the power of this gospel; the greatest power to take away the sincerity and purity of the Corinthians by corrupting their thoughts with other ideas that are not from God and lies that seem like the truth. Second Corinthians 11:2[48] states, "For I am jealous for you with godly jealousy. For I have betrothed you to one husband, that I may present you as a chaste virgin to Christ."

Because of this, Satan corrupts their thoughts; he begs them not to change from sincerity and purity for Christ. He also expresses his concern. This was Satan's first plan to cast down humanity. He also deceived Eve by defiling her thought. Even today, Satan has corrupted the sincerity and purity of many people through his deceitful ways, and his main way of opposing the work of the gospel and the kingdom of God is by deceiving and defiling the saints from the true knowledge that God has revealed to them.

Eve was not wrong when she answered Satan's question. She had no intellectual disability. She did not have the problem of forgetting and being confused about what God said. However, we see that he corrupted her mind by distorting what God said. Satan did not wage any kind of

---

46 NKJV
47 KJV
48 NKJV

war to throw man away from such life and glory, but he only succeeded in perverting Eve's thoughts without using any special method.

Eve had the same issue. In other words, instead of living the life she was living by completely believing what God said, she accepted and coped with the incorrect understanding of Satan's concepts. What she was denied was little in comparison to what she was given. As a result, in order to fall from her glory, she replaced all the trees in the world with one tree. As the apostle Paul put it in 2 Corinthians 11:2, she inadvertently took away her virginity.

The term "virgin" denotes something unblemished, unadulterated, distinct, and pure. But now, at Satan's request, she took away that virgin intellect that had been entrusted solely to God. She lost her purity when she lost her virginity. One of the primary reasons God prohibited mankind from eating from the tree was to protect his virginity. This meant that man might live his life knowing that what God said and ordered was true. That tree distinguished between the good and the evil.

Man has a will, but his life is a creation that accepts only what God says as truth and lives with a pure conscience. Until that day, without giving a rational answer, he lived by believing only what God said. But now there is a question about what God has said. When this fruit was eaten, the person who created it to live in virginity (pure thought or faith) was forced to live by judging things by himself. Because of this, instead of living in purity (believing that God exists), it became his duty to distinguish between good and bad by giving reasons. Man was created to believe in God as the only truth that God has and to live sincerely. Ecclesiastes 7:29[49] states, "Lo, this only have I found, that God hath made man upright; but they have sought out many inventions." Man was not created for a philosophical mind but for an innocent mind. When he tries to live using his own rational mind instead of accepting God's truth sincerely, he descends to a place where he cannot come out.

Salvation and Mind

When the Lord Jesus gave Himself to pay the price for mankind, one of the things He paid for was to restore the virginity of the human

---

49 KJV

mind. When God redeemed us in Christ Jesus, He restored our salvation and made us enter that peace of mind. When the apostle Paul explained what could be the reason for a person's salvation, he stated in 1 Corinthians 1:20–21,[50] "Where is the disputer of this age? Has not God made foolish the wisdom of this world? For since, in the wisdom of God, the world through wisdom did not know God, it pleased God through the foolishness of the message preached to save those who believe."

The key phrase in this passage is "the foolishness of the message preached." The sermon is God's wisdom and truth revealed. However, salvation is contingent on the foolish acceptance of this fact. The fact that people are not saved when the gospel is preached in different places is not because our gospel has lost its power. This truth of the gospel works only when the fool receives it foolishly. God's wisdom is in creating a fool. In other words, because God conveyed the truth to the creature and the creature cannot grasp and accept it with its own intellect, the only solution is for the creature to accept foolishly what God has said.

God's main dilemma is that he cannot describe his magnificence and identity in any way that humanity can comprehend. This is why if a person foolishly believes and accepts without question the truth that God has revealed to him, his life and lifestyle will be altered. A man's blessing is dependent on his foolish faith. This is why, in His wisdom, God has made salvation easy and suited for everyone, so the topic of salvation is not too difficult to pass from the mind of man.

This is to foolishly accept the righteousness and eternal life that God has freely and graciously given through Jesus Christ without any work or action. But the biggest problem is trying to understand this knowledge with the human mind. The simplest way to pass over from death to life and eternal life is to know and believe that God is God and to accept what He says blindly.

To enter God's kingdom, a person puts aside his rationality or his own knowledge, and when he accepts what God has said without question and foolish faith, his foolishness is considered wisdom. He will be saved by being wise in his foolishness. In the New Testament, God established the first law that God gave to Adam again in a new form. God revealed

---

50 NKJV

His wonderful work of salvation to mankind in a way that seems foolish to man in a way that man cannot understand. What does a person need to be saved? It is only to accept God's good news truth with faith even if it is not understood by the mind.

One of the things that amaze me when people accept the Lord as their Savior is that they are born with such a virgin mind. As a result, amazing things begin to happen in the lives of these new believers. Their prayers will be answered shortly. They have no problem believing what they are told. But after a while, this virginity is corrupted by people who have been saved earlier, or because of the experience and weakness they face in life, Satan slowly takes that virgin and makes their faith weak. Instead of foolishly believing the Word of God, their lives will be ruined when they want to be rational. It is not possible to believe foolishly and live wisely.

Salvation comes from accepting God's foolish knowledge by faith. Man cannot understand things that cannot be seen or touched with the natural mind. Faith requires foolishness to believe something that cannot be understood by the human mind and something that is outside the law of creation.

God's Thought and Human Mind

The life and livelihood of a human being is determined only by the knowledge and truth in his mind. Man can transcend the great purpose for which he was created and the potential power within him. But to do this, he must accept and believe God's knowledge and truth in his mind daily. As long as he does this, it will be easy to live a life full of power and grace for the glory of God and happiness of mankind. Only the knowledge and truth of God instilled in the human mind provide the greatest power and cause to live the purpose of life. The reason for living a good or poor life, success or failure, is knowledge in the mind.

The greatest tool that God has used in all His dealings with man since the time of Adam is sharing His thoughts. We find God's idea in the Word holding the highest place. God has conveyed His thoughts through holy prophets and apostles in the past. The reason He even gave the Holy Word was to share His thoughts with people.

When we read the Word, God's main purpose is not to give words but to make us understand the thoughts in the Word. When we say that God spoke, we mean that He expressed His thoughts. There is nothing created or living on earth or in heaven that is not in the mind of God. Even when He fulfilled the cause of our salvation, as James puts it, "of his own will he brought us forth by the word of truth" (James 1:18).

His ultimate goal is for everything to be according to His thoughts and counsel. When we read or study God's Word, the biggest reason is to understand what God's intention is in that word. We study God's Word to know God's thoughts. Christianity is basically accepting and believing the thought of God foolishly and living that thought. Anything other than that is pointless and purposeless.

In Acts 13:36[51] it says, "For David, after he had served the purpose of God in his own generation." When Luke summarizes David's life in one verse, he closes it by saying, "Serve God's thoughts and sleep." He killed Goliath because that was God's will. The great victory of life and ministry that David's reign brought in the land of Israel was because it was God's plan. The Holy Spirit's summary of David's life is not about what he did but rather about the purpose he served. A man can accomplish many things in his day; the question is not what he did but whose purpose he served.

The fundamental reason God protected, anointed, and utilized David to ensure his survival was that David carried God's thought. King Saul was mighty and a warrior. However, Saul hurled a spear at David and missed him twice. If he had hit him with his sword, he would have destroyed not only David but also the plan of God in David.

Even after we are saved, we are allowed to live because it is God's great desire and concept to fulfill the plan that He placed in us in Christ Jesus. Knowing God's thought and wisdom implies understanding why God has given us health, jobs, marriage, money, and other necessities for life on earth. It is the will and thought of God we carry and live by that makes us successful.

---

51 AMP

There is no big or small, rich or poor, successful or unsuccessful person on this earth. But big mind or small, rich mind or poor, successful or unsuccessful spiritual or physical mind, as a man thinks, so he is.

Part Two

Chapter 4—The Human Mind from a Scientific Point of View

Daniel 12:4,[52] "Many shall run to and fro,
and knowledge shall increase."

Civilization and the Bible

God, the first owner of civilization and knowledge, introduced knowledge to mankind in the book of Genesis. It was God Himself who designed a ship that could carry Noah and his family as well as all the animals of the earth two by two. Although it took Noah forty years to build the ark, it was flawless in terms of civilization.

God revealed not just the design of the ark but also the design of Moses' tent and the incredible items contained therein. Furthermore, it was He who taught Bezalel a craft in order for them to acquire the knowledge and expertise required for the design. Later, when David considered changing from a tent to a temple, it was God Himself who provided the plan. God is not opposed to civilization. Rather, He promotes civilization by demonstrating and imparting knowledge. Man's civilization has been used for evil, revolt, and devastation, yet the beginning was good and beneficial in God's eyes.

God gave civilization and knowledge to man by giving knowledge to man's mind and intelligence and wisdom to his profession. If there was no human mind, there would be no civilization. Although the source of civilization is God, it is an undeniable fact that the human mind is the main tool created by God.

---

52 NKJV

One of God's greatest gifts to mankind is intellectual creativity. All the knowledge and teachings that we see today are the research skills that have come from the use of the God-given mind. Although there is no one who created everything except God, it is true that God allowed man to create his own world among the creatures He created. When we say man created, we don't mean that he brought something that didn't exist, but he used his intelligence to create new ideas and show his work of art.

To understand this, we have to see the big difference between humans and animals. Since the creation of man, he has been able to change the world he lives in with his creativity in ways that cannot be imagined. Although there are many fields where human beings have improved their lives by using their minds, it will be useful to see where human life has come from so far.

The man who lived in a cave today has been able to make very beautiful and magnificent dwellings. Apart from his residence, he has built buildings that are amazing in their size and height to the extent that it is hard to believe that human hands have built this. When we study the construction of the world's largest and tallest building, we can see and know how big the seemingly small human mind is.

One of the tallest buildings in the world is in Dubai, and this building is called Burj Khalifa. This building cost 1.5 billion dollars. Its height is 2,722 feet, and it has 154 floors. It also has two levels of underground parking. This amazing building has 30 thousand houses and nine hotels. The building work started on January 6, 2004, and was completed six years later, on December 30, 2009. It has fifty-seven elevators, and each elevator can hold twelve to fourteen people. It has eight electric escalators (https://en.wikipedia.org/wiki/Burj_Khalifa).

We have seen advances in travel from the time when man started to travel on the back of a horse. Today we see airplanes flying at 3,500 kilometers per hour or 1100 miles per hour. Planes fly at an altitude of 75,000 feet. It takes just one hour and fifty-five minutes to travel from New York to London. The fastest train built in Japan goes 374 miles per hour. Other wonderful creations of the human mind that have amazed the world today are driving cars, amazing road works, the development of the telephone, and the evolution of the internet. Although the human mind is very small in size and weight, it is the same human mind that controls and governs all creation in his world (https://www.travelandle-isure.com/trip-ideas/bus-train/fastest-trains-in-the-world).

The Creation of the Human Mind from a Scientific Point of View

Our mind is one of the parts of our body, and it is a complex and wonderful work that God created in a way that is far more elaborate than any other part of our body. Although it may be small on the outside, what is inside and what it can do is more than the mind itself can imagine.

When the human head is weighed, it weighs an average of three pounds or one point five kilograms, which is only 2 percent of the total body weight. An elephant's head, one of the largest animals in the world, weighs only 2 percent of its body weight. This means that humans have a larger head size compared to their larger body size.

If the blood vessels in a person's head were stretched like a thread, it would be 100,000 miles. There are 100 billion neurons in our brain, and there are 1,000 to 10,000 synapses for each neuron. As long as a person uses his brain properly, new neurons are being created throughout his life. The speed at which information travels through our brain is 268 miles per hour. It is amazing how quickly information moves through the mind when a person is speaking or thinking. Before we even start to think and start to say what we think, the information that is arranged in our mind is overwhelming and hard to think about (https://www. youtube.com/watch?v=DxLpd2XE1KI).

The head is only 2 percent of the weight of a person's whole body, but our head uses 20 percent of the energy our body produces and the oxygen it takes. Seventy-five percent of our head is water. Although we are surprised to think that the creation and ability of the human mind are so great, scientists say that we are using less than 10 percent of the mental ability that God has given to man. Although scientists cannot say why this happens, if what they say is correct and true, according to the Word of God, it is not difficult to imagine that man lost 90 percent after the fall of sin.

It is said that only 5 percent of society used their mind to introduce the great discoveries of civilization. If this is true, it shows that the majority of the population is not using their mind as they should. It is also not difficult to imagine the change that our world can see if the other 95 percent of society starts to use their mind.

It is a great loss that 95 percent of society is a beneficiary of the discoveries made by the 5 percent of society who use their mind. It is very important to encourage both children and adults to use their minds in every church and school. This is one of the purposes of this book. Our mind is the greatest resource God has given us. By using and taking great care of this wonderful gift, we can use our talents to change our own lives and be a great blessing to God's kingdom and the world.

The Ability to Use the Human Mind and Creativity

Every child is born with creativity. Scientists who study children's brains say that 95 percent of children between the ages of two and four are born with high levels of creativity. These children have a high ability to dream, create, ask questions, try everything, and make pictures. But when these same children reach the age of seven, their creativity drops from 95 percent to 4 percent.

During the ages of four to seven, children are constantly being negatively influenced by their family and environment, thus preventing them from using their talents. Due to the pressure they are subjected to, they are forced to live using only a small amount of their mental potential. Because they are taught by their parents and/or society that they cannot do it, these youngsters are punished for being able to utilize their minds by making decisions based on the wishes and considerations of their surroundings and parents. That makes their dreams gloomier.

The main cause of children's misdeeds is their excitement and desire to try new things. They have no concept that it is impossible. Furthermore, because they are still young, they cannot discriminate between things that are good for them and things that are bad for them, which allows them to injure others and make mistakes. However, they have a drive to know and learn rather than to damage or do evil. When parents take action to fix what they perceive to be an error, they disregard their children's curiosity, drive to learn, optimism, and courage.

The spirit of potential, tasting, touching, knowing, and inquiry that was bestowed on them at the time of their creation in their inner consciousness decreases from 95 percent to 4 percent at this moment. When youngsters are informed that something is impossible or not feasible more than a hundred and fifty thousand times before they turn seventeen, according to studies, they respond with "yeah" or "okay" just only five thousand times.

How much more proof is needed to show that society can destroy the creative minds of children with negative speech? Yes, negative talk can crush children's minds; positive speech can also make them grow. In my view, fighting and eradicating this social culture that destroys the human mind should be the main priority of families, national leaders, and religious leaders. I am convinced that achieving this goal would not only make the world more colorful and creative but would also significantly aid in the development of morally upright families and societies.

There is the law of use in our mind. This usage rule is called "use it or lose it." If we don't use our mind as it should be used, it will be lethargic and lazy to create, work, and move; however, if creativity gets a chance to take off, it has the potential to be beneficial.

Our mind is given to us to serve us as long as we use it and work with it. But if we are not willing to use our brains and do not act on them, they will sit and sleep. It is said that no one can make the bed while sitting in bed; no one can change his life without using his mind. This is why I say there is no lazy person but a lazy mind. There is no poor man but a poor mind. There is no ignorant person but an ignorant mind.

When God created man, God gave man a mind that could do all of these things rather than give him riches, knowledge, or talents. The mind is where knowledge and expertise have their home. Many families only observe that their kids attend school without making any effort to learn more about their kids' modes of thought. Because of this, youngsters learn the alphabet but do not acquire the mental abilities necessary for life, leading them to become losers and dejected or lacking in direction as adults. They only learned the lessons taught in school and not the skills of living.

A passage in Proverbs says, "Train up a child in the way he should go [teaching him to seek God's wisdom and will for his abilities and talents], Even when he is old, he will not depart from it" (Proverbs 22:6).[53] Other translations use the word "lead" with the ideas of "coach," "teach," and "train." If a child is taught as a young child and meets someone who exemplifies and practices the appropriate method, he will not be able to turn his back on his training as an adult or even later in life. More than simply the alphabet is taught here. Even as he becomes older, the manner of life he was raised in prevents him from straying from what he was taught and prepared for. A thought pattern will persist in its current form for the duration of its existence.

Improper use of the mind is a big problem that can be seen in society as well as in the church. If there is a right and healthy mind, it is easier to establish a right and healthy society and a healthy church. There are many rich minds born from poor families. There are many brilliant minds born from uneducated families. If he gets a chance and helps a person to use his mind, the mind is a great resource that is given without discrimination on this earth.

The mind must be used in order to apply expertise. Every person is born with the capacity to create. The difference is that some people don't acknowledge their creativity, while others give themselves permission to think that it can be done with the crazy ideas and visions that come to them, and they work with passion to make it happen.

The Mind and the Civilized World

When we live in the world, whether we like it or not, people respect or despise us according to our ability to use our mind. Someone who is big on the mind is always in demand. Life does not care whether we are thin or fat, short or tall, white or black. But life extends a hand and accepts a person who is big in mind. The amount of payment or salary that is paid to us in any office is determined by the knowledge and skills of our mind. Our pay usually reflects what we can do in our minds, not who we are in human terms.

---

53 AMP

God's and man's respect for a person depends on the quality and size of the person's thoughts and ideas and knowledge in his mind. God saw man's heart and caused him to regret his creation because of man's mind and desires. Genesis 6:5[54] states, "The LORD saw that the wickedness (depravity) of man was great on the earth, and that every imagination or intent of the thoughts of his heart were only evil continually." It is not poverty or wealth that makes God sad for man. But the thoughts and desires of his heart were evil, so he repented. Finally, we see him destroy it with water. If the mind is not good, there is no good life. The knowledge and what is in the mind makes a person great, small, noble, humiliated, evil or good.

In Proverbs 20:5,[55] there is a passage that says, "A plan (motive, wise counsel) in the heart of a man is like water in a deep well, but a man of understanding draws it out." God's thoughts for each person are deep and many. Everyone is blessed with ideas. As the Bible says, there are many thoughts in the human heart. No one pays or goes to school for ideas. However, ideas are like deep water and need to be drawn out. Anyone who uses their mind, as long as the ideas are good and quality, there is no one who does not want to respect that person.

Everyone can go deep and draw out. We will return to this idea in another chapter. However, what I want to bring up here is that people create or see something unseen; the difference is that some people dig deep and use it while others fail to do so. Sometimes when we look at children, we see that they say or think things that are beyond their age; this is not what they have gained through knowledge and experience, but they say without even noticing by drawing out from God's creative ideas for all people. There is a saying in Ethiopia that a child's things are two fruits: one is ripe, and the other is raw. Sometimes we see children surprising us with amazing answers and questions, and sometimes they say and do childish things.

I once heard such a story. A truck passing under a bridge got stuck and was unable to continue. Local law enforcement and tow trucks tried to pull the truck out but were unable to get it free. A child asked

---

54 AMP
55 AMP

the traffic police what the problem was. When the officer explained to the child what had happened, the child looked around and immediately suggested that if the truck's tires were inflated a little, the truck would be able to move. The traffic officer immediately removed the truck using the advice given by the child. We can see from this boy that great ideas don't always come from great people.

The main message I want to convey in this chapter is that our mind is a great resource given to us by God to create, change, dream, and plan. In the following chapters, we will see a few ways in which we can use our mind to answer the question of how we can use this mind for the benefit of God's kingdom and the blessing of the earth.

Chapter 5—The Human Mind and the Law of Creation

Romans 7:1,[56] "The Law has jurisdiction [to rule]
over a person as long as he lives?"

The earth has been given over to man. God created man to govern the planet, not to live with his heart occupied by things on earth. Mankind's downfall began when man was ruled by creation that was given to him to rule and when he pursued happiness from what was created for him to enjoy.

The main purpose of man's creation is to know, worship, and constantly seek God. However, instead of seeking God, man sought something that God had grown on earth and was forbidden from touching. As a result, the animals he was controlling rebelled against him and left his leadership.

Because the planet and everything on it was given to man, his sole interaction with this world was to know the law to accomplish what he wanted by believing this. We should not beg for something that belongs to us. It is our part to know how the law of nature works and live according to the law. The earth was turned over to Satan's realm when Adam and Eve lost this immense power and dignity, so humanity could not exercise its power. That is why our Lord Jesus referred to Satan as the ruler of this world.

The world is dominated by Satan, but the earth is still governed by God's preordained rules. If a person is right with God and has this belief in his heart, he will be able to achieve what he desires. The rules of creation cannot be broken by Satan. If he breaches it, it is only for a short period and to the extent permitted in a specific location. As a result, if a person works in accordance with the rules that God has established on earth, everything will go as planned. Furthermore, as Christians, we

56 AMP

now have more authority and power in Christ than Satan does. But we can only wield our power if we understand natural and spiritual laws and put them into action.

The apostle Paul said in 1 Corinthians 3:21–23[57]:

So let no one boast in men [about their wisdom, or of having this or that one as a leader]. For all things are yours, whether Paul or Apollos or Cephas (Peter) or the world or life or death or things present or things to come; all things are yours, and you belong to Christ; and Christ belongs to God.

It's incredible that all is ours. If there is a language and prayer that is not fitting in the kingdom of heaven, it is when someone begs for and desires what he has. Many people's prayers go unanswered because they ask for what God has given them and what is rightfully theirs.

The spiritual world allows us to begin with what we have rather than what we lack. Everything belongs to us. In Christ, God has given us everything. If a person lives his life with this perspective every day, he will be happy and productive. The challenge is how to use what I have rather than how to obtain it. Romans 8:32[58] states, "He who did not spare [even] His own Son, but gave Him up for us all, how will He not also, along with Him, graciously give us all things?" When he says everything with him, he means everything as we all know. Today, the solution to any of our life's questions is at our fingertips. The problem is that we do not believe reality, yet in this reality, we own everything. Everything is mine. Hallelujah.

In 1 Corinthians 1:5[59] it says, "In every thing ye are enriched by him, in all utterance, and in all knowledge." This verse was written to the Corinthians, who had many problems and spiritual decline. For those Christians who failed to live according to what was written for them, even if we think about how this can happen, the reality is the same. Paul will enter into correction by reviving the identity that was given to them when they believed in Christ. Our life experiences and struggles should not change who we are.

---

57 AMP
58 AMP
59 KJV

Trying to do and doing are different. The person who tries to do it is trying to bring what he doesn't have. But a person who has been made already is not supposed to try, seek, and pray but live. A person who is rich in words and knowledge in all things should think and speak like a rich man and live like a rich man in all things.

In Psalm 23:1[60] it is written, "The Lord is my shepherd, I shall not want." He says that he trusts the Shepherd so that his desire is nothing but God until his desire for something else disappears. David's success was not in running to get what he didn't have but in knowing that all that God had was his and that he had nothing to lose or want. This is one of the secrets that made David great. David desired to be king, but David did not want the throne. He spent the next twenty-one years traveling through caverns and deserts without once praying for the throne. Nothing else was lacking, and what he needed was not what he desired but rather a shepherd at his side to guide him in the direction he desired.

Living outside of this spirit causes a person to develop jealousy, greed, robbery, fear, and anxiety. These issues are not the result of a lack of resources but rather of our ignorance of them. We have everything we need nearby. It is in our control. The freedom that comes from accepting this and acting accordingly is enormous. There should be nothing I seek, but things should seek me. Anything I desire is something I own. Everything that is mine is in me through Christ. That's why when I talk about will or desire, I say that the biggest job a person has is to consciously decide what they want rather than try to make it happen. Not because work is not needed but because the spirit in which I work is essential. Working knowing that I have it and working to get it are different. To live knowing who we are and living to get something are as far apart as heaven and earth.

Proverbs 4:23[61] states, "Keep thy heart with all diligence; for out of it are the issues of life." King Solomon knew that the source of life was in the inner well of man. Even though he had brothers before and above him, who were worthy of the throne according to the law, the throne came knocking at the door of his house. Absalom sought the throne through deceit and Amnon through rebellion. Both were beautiful and

---

60 KJV
61 KJV

had good things in them. But their problem was that when they wanted the throne by force, they fell short before finding it.

Life flows from the inside out, not from the outside in. There should not be anything that we seek and find, but things should seek and find us. Matthew 6:33[62] says, "But seek ye first the kingdom of God, and his righteousness; and all these things shall be added unto you." As we have seen since the beginning of mankind, before God created Adam and Eve, it took him about six days to create the world for Adam and Eve. This means that what is prepared for man to be created is not in moderation but in an extreme form.

Looking back now, I am amazed at the preparations we made before the birth of our first child. I remember the preparations we made for a newborn child who knew nothing was beyond the child's ability and needs. After all, everything was done for the child, but the joy was ours. As a parent prepares for a child's needs before they are even born, God also prepares for His children to provide everything they will need in life.

Peaceful living is everyone's destiny. Life begins with rest, not effort. A person who rests for work is much better than who works to rest. For nothing we have done can make us rest. God began life for Adam and Eve by preparing everything for them, including food. It says in Genesis, "And the LORD God commanded the man, saying, 'You may freely (unconditionally) eat [the fruit] from every tree of the garden'" (Genesis 2:16).[63]

Even if there is something we think we don't have, compared to what we do have, the distance between what we have is like heaven and earth. When God forbade Adam and Eve to eat from just one tree, He allowed them to eat from every tree in Eden. If we focus on what we have, we know that even what we don't have is small compared to what we have. How many are not satisfied with what they have?

It is foolish to focus on God's gift when he has given us everything and is the One who created it. Even if we claim to have nothing in our hands, the Lord will provide us with what we require when we require it and in the manner He desires. Life will undoubtedly provide its table

---

62 KJV
63 AMP

to someone who has a firm belief in this concept. Whatever is mine, it is in me. I am the only one who can bring that out of me. This should be a true reflection of the believer.

The human heart (mind) is like a source.

Since the human mind is like a source, it is important to study and know about the mind. The source of life is in the thoughts of man. This is why when the Lord Jesus spoke about this matter, He said, "Evil things come out of the heart of an evil person; from the heart of a good person come good things." Both good and evil come from the heart. It does not say that what is outside makes a person good or bad. Matthew 15:18[64] states, "But the things that come out of a person's mouth come from the heart, and these defile them."

Evil thoughts, murder, fornication, adultery, theft, false witness, and slander arise from the heart; these are the ones that defile a person. Everything originates from the human heart. Its source is in the human heart. Not what a person says or does. We are what we are because of the source. If we change bad thoughts with good thoughts, our heart becomes a source of good things. This is the message of the Lord Jesus in Matthew 15:18–19. It is your inner thoughts that determine your actions. It is the thought in your heart that creates what you see in your outer life.

If a person thinks evil, he has a high capacity to do evil. A person who thinks good things has the same capacity to do good things. What we need is inside us, not outside. Everything that happens outside, whether good or bad, comes from within. When I say this, I am not saying that evil people cannot do evil to us or that evil cannot happen to us. But to say that everything that happens in my life because of me is determined only by the good or bad thought that is in me.

It says in Micah 2:1,[65] "Woe to those who devise wickedness and work evil on their beds! When the morning dawns, they perform it, because it is in the power of their hand." All it takes to do evil is to stir it up. It is within man that he has the power to do evil. What brings evil out of a person is to contemplate. This means that evil is planned and done in the human heart or human mind. As we saw in Proverbs 20:5, meditation

64 NIV
65 ESV

is a process of recording from deep. As much as we put into it, good or bad things will come out.

Power is not in action but in thought. If people want the energy to act, they need time to think. Usually evil or good, blessing or curse, disease or health, wealth or poverty starts from the thought, which is the inner power of man. For the source of all things is in the mind of human thought.

To be able to think rightly is to have the power to live rightly. A man should not labor for work but for thought. Change and success come from the power of deep thought, not the result of effort and fatigue. Work is the product of thought. It is worth working for. A work done without thought is labor. A person who can think has the ability to work hard.

When we say that life flows from the inside to the outside, we mean that everything begins with human thought. A man who is careful about his thoughts is careful about his life. Holiness does not begin with actions but with thoughts. Generosity is the result of thought, not action. What we see in our life is what we think. The easiest way to change your life is to change your mind. Behavioral change begins with thoughts, not actions. If a person thought more than he worked hard, he would have more energy to do what he wanted.

The amount of power of an electric generator is determined by the amount of water it has stored, and the power of a person to be and do something great in life is determined by the time he gives to think. A lot of thought generates a lot of power. A little thought, a little power. The type and quality of the thought determines the type and quality of the life.

Knowing about prayer and meditating on it with the help of the Holy Spirit are required to be a man of prayer. God will give us the grace to pay attention and be as much as we think. It is absurd to change our spiritual life without our thoughts. Colossians 3:2[66] says, "Set your mind and keep focused habitually on the things above [the heavenly things], not on things that are on the earth [which have only temporal value]." Consider what this passage says. It's a formal expression of focus in your mind. If we give attention to something spiritual in our mind and think about it in a habitual way, we will get the ability to live that spiritual

66 AMP

life. That is what gives us the opportunity to live in purity and for all our organs to serve as weapons of righteousness. There will be no power to prevent us from living that kind of life.

Spiritual results for those who think about spiritual things will inevitably produce physical results for those who think about physical things. When we say that everything is ours, we mean that everything is in us. But the way to bring out what is inside us is to believe and habitually meditate that everything in us will bring it out from the big source. For as a man thinks, so is he.

Chapter 6—The Four Parts of the Human Mind

Romans 12:2,[67] "Be transformed and progressively changed [as you mature spiritually] by the renewing of your mind [focusing on godly values and ethical attitudes]."

A human mind consists of four things: (1) the place where we handle thoughts; (2) our memory, where we store our thoughts; (3) image, where we create images; and (4) our conscience, where our faith and conscience are made. We will look at these four things in turn, but before that, let's analyze these four in turn and see how they work together so that it becomes clear to us.

These four things take place in a person's mind before a person gains any insight, makes a decision, and takes action in his life. These are the things that a person thinks willingly with his conscience (emphasize the word willingly) because all the thoughts that come to our mind do not go directly to our memory. All thoughts that a person thinks of willingly will be recorded or saved by entering the memory section.

What I mean by this is not to say that there are no things that pass through our minds and enter our memory compartments without our permission. This is because if we hear and see something repeatedly without realizing it, our mind can register them without us knowing it. The reason why I want to strengthen our will is that if we declare that we do not want any idea to enter our thoughts, if we turn our attention away from that thing, there will be no thoughts that enter into us.

When our mental part, which is the creator of the image of the many ideas stored in the memory, creates an image by organizing the ideas, we get an understanding in our fourth part, or we get an understanding of what we thought about and the image we saw. That image created in our

67 AMP

mind becomes our reality. It means that before we do or say anything, it will be the standard for what we say or what we set out to do.

In other words, if we made an image, it means we knew or believed. Or it means that we accepted it as right and responded to everything in life. According to this idea, a person's behavior, decision, attitude, feeling, and action will be determined only according to the image in the person and the reality and perception created because of the image.

If we go back words with this idea, everything that a person believes and lives or what he does in the visible world is based on what he accepts as truth in the mind. What makes him accept this as true is because of an image in his mind. This image is created in our subconscious mind. Our subconscious mind processes all the ideas stored in our memory bank and creates an image. Everything that is stored in this reservoir of thoughts is taken from the part of our mind that handles thoughts that are in our conscious mind.

In the world of communication, many people fail to communicate and say the same words; differences or conflicts arise because of the image in each person's mind and the understanding created by the image. The words and the images that are spoken differ from person to person. There is communication between two people's words only as long as they have the same image or understanding about that word or idea. If the words are the same, but the picture is different, it is impossible to communicate. This is one of the biggest differences between couples in a marriage. Attitudes, understandings, and meanings between women and men are far apart. If they both don't talk about their image, there will always be misunderstanding and disagreements.

Conscious Mind and Subconscious Mind

The human brain is divided into two main parts. One is called conscious, and the other is called subconscious. Our conscience is the main and primary part of our mind that decides whether any idea is right or not. This section does three basic things: (1) it is the reason-giving part of the mind, (2) the selective (choices) part of the mind, and (3) the decisive (decisions) part of the mind.

Our subconscious mind doesn't reason; it doesn't choose, and it doesn't decide. But it takes whatever we have processed in our conscious mind, creates an image, and makes that the reality of our lives. In the human mind, from the initial thought to the consummation of the thought, our thought goes through at least three stages.

- Stage 1: *Internal energy* (Potential)—this is our natural self or our naturally gifted abilities and desires. Human thought is mostly related to the natural personality or natural ability. For example, an astronaut and a farmer differ in their ideas according to their natural inclinations. One thinks about the sky, and the other thinks about the ground.

- Stage 2: *Understanding*—this is where our mind takes the idea received from the outside and examines it and tries to relate and adapt the idea to its own world.

- Stage 3: *Realization*—this stage is what makes us take action by understanding the original idea.

Four Basic Facts of the World of Thought

- *It is difficult to change an idea that is once established in the mind.* Our intelligence and the type of thoughts we have are our God-given innate abilities within us. It takes time for our brains to accept something as true. But it takes a long time to change what we once accepted as true. This is why it is difficult to change an idea once established in a person's life. The first six years of a child's life are especially critical; in this age group, it will not be easy to change the idea that family and society have asserted that all their life experiences and what they have said are accepted as true. The basis of social culture, tradition, and rules is the mindset that is passed from parent to child.

- *Each person is completely unique in thought.* Just as human fingerprints are not alike, so are human thoughts. It is like DNA that differentiates our personalities and physical abilities from each other. Each person is different not only in thought but also in mentality. Everyone has their own unique mindset. It is for this reason that man's greatest lifework is to form fellowship with one another. If we say that two people have the same idea, it means that one of them has influenced the other or that one of them has changed his own idea by the other.

- *Each person's inclinations and needs are different and unrelated according to the difference in our thinking.* The biggest reason why our attitudes and thoughts are not alike and are different is that it is determined by the mentality or thoughts we think.

- *No one can break open and see the thoughts in a person's mind.* Just as we cannot enter a person's house unless that person opens the door and lets us enter, no one, including Satan, can see or know what is in a person's mind except God and the person himself. Because of this, no one can control our thoughts. Human thought is a great resource that God has given us to protect so that no one can control it and use it for their own needs. As I mentioned above, good or bad people can influence us and change our direction on life or our way of thinking; however, they do not do this by controlling our thoughts. When we want, we have the ability to reject even those who have influenced us. Now let's look at each of the four parts of the mind faculty in detail.

1. Our Thought Room

Our mind does not create thoughts, but it tries to get used to and accept ideas in the process according to our ability and understanding. The mind cannot generate thoughts, but it can choose thoughts. To make our choice, we take an action, which will be meditation, to make a decision by taking ideas from the ideas we have stored in our memory or storage room.

Although scientists have not clearly stated what it is that generates thoughts outside of the human mind, our Bible teaches that thoughts come to the human mind from two directions. One is from God, and the other is from Satan. For this reason, there is an evil intention, and there is also a good intention, according to the source. Evil thoughts come from Satan, and good thoughts come from God.

The human mind does not generate thoughts; it can make its own choices based on the desires of the body and the spirit. We can see this as a third thought, which is human thought. But this makes us choosers of ideas, not creators of ideas. For example, a baby does not have any thoughts in his mind as soon as he is born. However, as he grows older, he begins to think. But what he thinks is mostly determined by the environment he grew up in.

This shows us that the child does not generate ideas by himself but that the ideas he thinks are shaped by the environment. Based on what a child sees, hears, and learns from the surrounding society, he accepts and shapes his thinking with the judgment of his conscience. That's why we say children are like their father or like their mother. The father's behavior is reflected in the child because the father's thinking is imprinted on the child.

But when an idea comes from outside, it is sudden. We did not think about it before. It is not something we have generated by taking time to meditate. Knowing this is life changing because many people base their decisions without knowing the source of their thoughts. Any decision made without knowing the source of ideas can be dangerous and evil. Because one source of ideas is Satan. Before we think about any idea and come to a decision, it is very important to look at the source and origin of the idea.

When we look at Matthew 16:21–23, we see that Peter took the Lord Jesus and said, "May God forbid it"! The reason for this was that the Lord Jesus began to speak about His death. What Peter does in this passage is what we would think from anyone who says they are going to die. However, even though the idea seems like the person who cares is compassionate and loving, the way the Lord saw and handled this idea was different.

In verse 23,[68] we see him turning around and telling Peter, "Get behind Me, Satan! You are a stumbling block to Me; for you are not setting your mind on things of God, but on things of man." It is known that Satan does not have anything good of his own, and the words "don't die"

---

68 AMP

can never be found in Satan's vocabulary because the Bible calls him a murderer from the beginning.

Satan's approach was to thwart the purpose of the Lord's coming by acting on Peter's good intentions. That is why the Lord said that "you have become an obstacle for me." Some translations have interpreted the idea that "you have become an obstacle" to mean as "you have blocked my way." This signifies that Satan was aware that the Lord Jesus could only redeem mankind when He was dying on the cross and that the Lord was thus headed toward His own destruction. If the Lord had not opposed him by telling him to go, he would have thwarted God's great plan because his idea was not good. This is why it is said that every good idea is not God's idea. Likewise, in John 13:2[69] it states, "It was during supper, when the devil had already put [the thought of] betraying Jesus into the heart of Judas Iscariot, Simon's son." Before Satan possessed Judah, he first implanted his idea.

Judah was defeated when he entertained the idea. If Judah had discerned the idea and resisted the devil like Jesus, the end would have been different. Investigating and discerning the ideas that come to our hearts and accepting or rejecting them is our biggest task in life. It is the little thoughts that we allow to enter our mind that takes control of our actions after it grows.

Let's look at the three ideas mentioned above in Genesis chapters 2 and 3 at the beginning of mankind. Man has accepted and believed the good idea God had given him. God told him what he should do and should not do. He also accepted the result of death if he did not obey. His world was only that which he heard from God.

In chapter 3 we see Satan giving Eve a strange idea. Satan said to her, "If you eat from this tree, you will not die, but you will be like God." Mind you, all the ideas that have come up so far are from outside. The first is from God, and the second is from Satan. But now, since a man has the right to choose or the power of will, the basis for making the choice was to look at the tree. It was man's choice to see the tree either from God's words or from Satan's words. Neither God nor Satan had any influence on man's decision. Both gave Eve their own ideas about

---

69 AMP

each other's identity and purpose. But Eve's view of the tree was from Satan's point of view, and for the first time, a strange physical desire or longing arose in Eve.

This love of the flesh was Eve's idea and will, and man decided to satisfy his own carnal desire based on the idea that came to him from the outside (from Satan). When we study thought, we always look at action. Action precedes thought. Every action is based on a thought. Every thought originates either from God or from Satan. The result will be according to the thought.

2. Memory

This section is a record of thoughts in our mind; it is a storehouse where we can store and recall information. The information must be entered and recorded in advance to save or retrieve that information later. The registry records information, knowingly or unknowingly. We consciously record what we want to record by thinking and meditating repeatedly. Our mind records everything that we pay attention to, whether good or bad; this is mostly based on what we hear or see. Not only what we consciously remember but also what we don't pay attention to unconsciously; if we hear and see something repeatedly, our mind records everything.

Any information we record is sent to our conscious mind in two ways. When we start thinking about finding that information, it brings the information from our memory and organizes it for us. But the second one sends the information in the form of thoughts and images even if we don't want it every few minutes. It sends the thoughts that we often think more quickly to our consciousness. The information we collect will inevitably affect our daily lives for better or for worse.

This section records information in two ways. One is long term, and the other is short term. To remember what was recorded, we need a movement or a sign of what we are about to do. As soon as our mind receives the signal, it presents the desired information to our consciousness. If we think and cannot present the information to our consciousness, it means that none of the information has been recorded, or it has not been recorded correctly. Because of this, it cannot be brought to our consciousness.

Ability to Record Mental Information

The biggest computer or iPad memory available today, as of the time this book was being written, is 160 terabytes. The human brain, however, has about 2500 terabytes. This means it can store three million hours of television programs. According to the experts, the television would need to run nonstop for 300 years in order to play every television show. In other words, even if someone can pass on that intellect to their offspring and use it for more than three generations, they will no longer be able to do so. The reality is God gave us the capacity to remember, and that is incredible, but a lot of people do not make use of this wonderful skill (https://www.youtube.com/watch?v=DxLpd2XE1KI).

This part of our mind is very important. Any image that is created in our mind and then understood in our subconscious is information taken from this part. Who we are is shaped by the type of information we put into this space. If we are not careful about everything we see and hear, we can become the kind of people who record it in our memory. For this reason, we need to be aware of what kind of information we enter in our mind.

In Psalm 119:11[70], the psalmist said, "I have hidden your word in my heart that I might not sin against you." The best strategy to prevent him from sinning in his daily life is not to fight against the coming sin but to hide the word of God in the memory room so that he would not sin in advance. The Amplified Bible translation says, "Your word I have treasured and stored in my heart." This verse shows us that David hid God's word in his heart like a great treasure in which a great historical treasure is kept. Our life is protected by the thoughts we put in our heart. The power we get to not sin against God is from the word of God we have stored in our mind. The information in our memory not only helps us become what we want but also prevents us from becoming what we don't want.

Luke 2:19[71] says, "But Mary treasured all these things, giving careful thought to them *and* pondering them in her heart." The mother of the Lord Jesus had many good things said about her Son; she kept all

---

70 NIV
71 AMP

that in her heart. At some point, she was looking at what she had been waiting for taking it out of her heart. The problem of the people of Israel was forgetfulness. This was because they quickly forgot everything that God had done and said to them because they did not record it in their hearts. Because of this, a nation that came out of Egypt, which was a powerful country at the time, ended up dead in the desert, led by wonders and miracles.

If they had thought about the greatness of their God, their actions and their ways would have been victorious and glorious. But they died eating the life-giving manna because their hearts were filled with daily food and water. They were satisfied with their bodies but lean with their souls. The lean of the soul is worse than the flesh. Psalm 106:15[72] says, "He gave them their request; but sent leanness into their soul."

Just as the human body is built by the type of food it eats, so the human soul is built by the type of information it enters into its mind every day. The lack of living the life you want to live is a problem with the information in the memory, so we need to be careful about what information we enter and what we think about every day.

3. Our Imaging Room

Our image maker is one of the main parts of our mind. This part collects the information received from our conscious mind and converts it into an image. It gives us the ability to make images, dream, or see what is not yet and what we have not seen with our physical eyes. Some call this image or vision; others call it a waking dream. It is said that "a person gains education or his ability to understand things by seeing more than 75%."[73] This amazing part of our mind shows us the dreams of our life that we have not yet achieved as if they had happened. Imagery is the ability to visualize something in our mind that we cannot perceive with our five senses. It is our mind that can create feelings and things that have

---

72 KJV

73 Jeff Hurt. "Looking to Learn: Why Visuals Are So Important," https://velvetchainsaw.com/2012/03/01/looking-learn-why-visuals-so-important/#:~:text=The%20majority%20of%20scientific%20and,learning%20is%20through%20your%20vision.

never existed before. But when we see them, we shouldn't think they will happen in the future but should be in our hands right now.

The power of imagination is our ability to create. We have to visualize things before they happen in our lives. If this is the case, there is nothing that prevents us from seeing with our physical eyes what we have seen in our imagination.

Psychologists say that humans are eye minded or visually driven creatures. Everything we think, remember, and do is based on vision. When God created man, he wanted to meet Him through his eyes. We all have two eyes. One is what makes us see and understand external things, and the second is our inner eye, which helps us see the spiritual and intellectual world. When the Lord Jesus spoke about these two eyes, He explained that the Pharisees and Sadducees were people who only saw with their physical eyes and were blind with their inner eyes. Internal blindness is worse than external (https://velvetchainsaw.com/2012/03/01/looking-learn-why-visuals-so-).

Some people have enormous goals and have used their abilities to create many amazing works even though they are physically blind but have eyes on the inside. On the other hand, many people have healthy physical eyes but blind inner eyes. When a person is blinded within, his thoughts, speech, and all his life experiences testify to it. People who have nothing to live for but still live as if they do, who see life only for profit and not for purpose, who cannot live for others, who cannot surpass themselves, who have a lot of money or a lot of education but have no influence, are in their own prisons.

This is an issue of vision. Some people with enlightened inner eyes who come from underprivileged or ignorant backgrounds manage to break through and have the power and aptitude to inspire many by considering their thoughts and objectives.

A great skill of a leader is to see. His inner eye is enlightened and has the ability to lead the way and lead his followers to greater heights. The problem is that it is common to be cautious and turn off the eyes of the one who has many followers, but it is easy to do great work if an open-minded leader has followers. This is why the Lord Jesus said in

Matthew 15:14,[74] "Leave them alone; they are blind guides [leading blind followers]. If a blind man leads a blind man, both will fall into a pit." He demonstrated the risks of their blindness to the leader and follower.

King Solomon said in Proverbs 29:18,[75] "Where there is no vision [no revelation of God and His word], the people are unrestrained." Other meanings of the word "unrestrained" are self-control, loss, being out of control, loss of limits, and destruction. When someone loses their inner vision, they become disoriented, unable to manage themselves, and out of control.

The Word and its revelation are given to us by God in His great generosity so that our inner eyes may be enlightened and we may avoid falling into this type of spiritual crisis. In fact, one of the key reasons God speaks to us is so that we might see more than just what we hear. Psalm 89:19[76] says, "Once You spoke in a vision to Your godly ones," and Hosea 12:10[77] says, "I spoke to the prophets, gave them many visions and told parables through them." Whenever God speaks, we see that He wants His listeners to see what He is saying. Beyond that, as we see in Hosea, He gave more vision than the word.

In Jeremiah 1:9,[78] God touched Jeremiah's mouth and said, "I have put my word in your mouth." A little further down in the same chapter, in verse 11, God asked Jeremiah, "What do you see?" The reason for this is that although the power of the word that roots out and pulls down, destroys and throws down, builds and plants is placed in Jeremiah's mouth, if Jeremiah cannot perceive this word with his inner sight, God cannot do anything. But after Jeremiah said, "I see the branch of an almond tree," the Lord responded, "You have seen well, for I am [actively] watching over My word to fulfill it" (Jeremiah 1:11–12).[79]

We need to know how important our vision is. What we don't see is that no matter how much knowledge we have or how great the promise that God has spoken to us, it does not do anything good. It is not only

---

74 AMP
75 AMP
76 AMP
77 NIV
78 AMP
79 AMP

hearing the word but also seeing the word that makes us strive for the word that God has spoken to us. Basically, faith means being able to see what God has said. If people hear a word and cannot believe, it means that they cannot see with their inner eyes. As it is said, "If you can see, the invisible God can do the impossible."

Vision and Action

When we see God's character through vision, if we ask how He created the vast world from nothing before the world was created, we realize that the answer is because He saw the invisible and called it. Regarding this matter, the psalmist David says in Psalm 139:14–16[80] about His creation, "Your eyes saw my unformed body." The psalmist declares, "You created me because you saw something that had not yet been created." Isaiah 46:9–10[81] says, "Remember the former things, those of long ago; I am God, and there is no other; I am God, and there is none like me. I make known the end from the beginning, from ancient times, what is still to come. I say, 'My purpose will stand, and I will do all that I please.'" First, saying the last means that it is finished before it has even begun. This means that if it ends before it starts, it ends when it starts. If we ask how this is possible, the answer is short and clear. It means that He has already thought about what He intends to do or has seen the end of it before He has even started it.

It is enough to see one building work to understand this idea easily. Before the building is built, the builders draw a picture of what the building will look like when it is finished and put it on a large scale. The doors, the windows, the width of the rooms, their length are made on paper and placed in a blueprint; even the color of the building is drawn and displayed on a large board. Amazingly, when the building is finished, it ends up looking just like the original picture.

And so is human life. The greatest work is not to do what we want; the biggest task is to sit down and think about what we want to do and finish the picture. The problem with many people is that they live their lives with a missing or unfinished picture. People's confusion and getting lost in the middle of the road is not finishing the drawing. They learn

80 NIV
81 NIV

about academics, not what they want to be. They work, but they don't know what they are working for. They serve, but they do not know what results they serve to see. Life without a picture is a mess. It is not content; it bothers others and itself.

I don't believe anyone should be a mercenary. A mercenary is someone who works as a wage earner for someone else who has a vision or who has completed the image. This man lives to earn a salary, not to finish the homework of life that God has given him to do in his life. For this reason, he works but does not see any results or gets paid for working for what the other person sees, but he does not share in the results.

There is no shame in being employed. But it is sad to end the age for that. A person who works for a job should be able to prepare himself to live for what God has set before the creation of the world to work in him, but if he lives for that all his life, then this person's life is wasted. The mistake is not being employed; the mistake is not being able to see the life you were called to live while working in one place. Everyone has an inner eye. If he sees this with his eyes, if he begins to see what is not visible with his invisible eyes, that's when he begins to find his purpose in life and something to live for.

Abraham and His Vision

God's promise to give Abraham a son was true, and no one could stop him. Abraham's problem was that he did not see what God intended to give him. From the twelfth chapter of Genesis, the Lord not only told him repeatedly that He would not only give him a son but that his seed would inherit the nations, and even the kings of the world would come out and make him a blessing to the people of the world. God saw about Abraham children of flesh and spirit as numerous as the sand of the earth and the stars of the sky. But Abraham saw Eliezer. And beyond Eliezer, his request was for a son.

To change this situation, the Lord had to take Abraham out of his narrow tent and show him the stars of the sky and the sand of the earth. When Abraham began to see that God saw, then he believed God, and it was counted to him as righteousness. And the writer of Hebrews in chapter 11:12[82] says, "So from one man, though he was [physically] as good as dead, were born as many descendants as the stars of heaven in number, and innumerable as the sand on the seashore." Hallelujah. Our status quo doesn't mean anything. Not only was he able to remain childless, but his and Sarah's age of childbearing was not a problem. A person who can see what God has shown with his inner eyes will see not one but a blessing like many stars. If we see the picture inside, we are sure to see it in the outside world.

In Genesis 13:14–15[83] it is written, "And the Lord said to Abram, after Lot had separated from him: 'Lift your eyes now and look from the place where you are—northward, southward, eastward, and westward; for all the land which you see I give to you and your descendants forever.'" God's promise was true, but Abraham's vision was very important also because he could only inherit what he saw. He ordered that the direction of sight should be toward the four corners, for according to his sight, his inheritance endures. At this time, Abraham did two things. First, he saw, and second, he pulled his tent from the place where he was to inherit the land that God said he would inherit. To inherit what he saw, he had to tear down his tent and go to what he saw and trample the land.

Even today, life is like that. If we do not see it with our inner eye, there is nothing we can inherit. For we inherit only what we see. Many people's problem is that they can't see beyond the tent and can't tear the tent down. Their sight does not go beyond the tent. It is narrow. If we give time to our inner eye and try to see, the horizon is wide. There is no limit. The limit is as far as we can see. As it was said to Abraham, it is possible to see and go north, south, east, and west. Our limits and borders are like the horizon of our vision. We may have less time and age to complete all that we have seen, but the work to be done and the inheritance to be inherited can never be reduced. There is a lot of work left for our children if we do not finish it.

I think this is why most people's lives are wasted. The problem with the culture of misusing time is a lack of vision. I may be short on time, but I have never run out of work to do. Because of this, every minute

---

82 AMP
83 NKJV

and second is important and valuable to me. If it is not to rest my tired body or to prepare myself for other work, my rest is in the work I am doing. The desire of a person who sees is to see his dream come true. To a person who has a dream, diligence and hard work are their relatives.

4. Conscious and Subconscious Mind

Conscious Mind

Our conscious mind is the part of our mind that is responsible for everything we do consciously. On the other hand, it is also known as the gate or guardian. It is responsible for investigating and verifying any information that comes to our mind. Our conscious mind has three basic functions. As we saw above, our conscious is created to:

- Reason
- Choose
- Decide

When an idea comes to a person, our conscience looks for a good reason to accept the idea. And after finding sufficient reason, he chooses. The choice is either to accept or not to accept. In the third stage, when the reason chooses what it believes to be satisfactory, it decides, enters the idea, and goes through an important process to make it its own. At this time, the idea that has been directly selected and accepted by decision will be sent to the mental part of the memory or image storage and will be stored.

This ability to choose and decide with conscience is a great gift that God has given to mankind. Not even the idea that came from somewhere else, even the idea of God, the Creator of the mind, made him do anything without the will of the mind. When God shares His ideas, no matter how useful and important they are, He offers people to choose to accept them. He puts it before others so they can accept it and make a rational choice. He never sends His thoughts to someone by forcing them. What a noble creature man is! Even if the idea is right or wrong, saved or destroyed, it is based on their conscience; they are lucky to have the gift of will, which allows them to make decisions that are solely their own. This is God's eternal law and free gift to man.

In Deuteronomy 30:19,[84] it declares, "I call heaven and earth as witnesses against you today, that I have set before you, life and death, the blessing and the curse; therefore, you shall choose life in order that you may live, you and your descendants." He called heaven and earth as witnesses when He said, "I have set life and death, blessing and cursing, before you." When God gave man this great blessing, He gave him the conscience to be able to reason and distinguish good from evil, so He gave him the will to choose life or even death if he wanted to. Whether it is right or wrong, life is a human choice.

Conscience and Balance of Conscience

Conscience has balance. This is God's universal gift to all mankind. Every man is endowed with a balanced conscience. This helps us distinguish between what is moral and what is not. Not only does it identify, but it also prevents us from doing what is wrong. And when we go against the voice of our conscience, it passes judgment on our soul. This judgment makes us feel unpleasant feelings of sadness or guilt about the mistake we have made.

God gave man a conscience to guide him and to protect him. If we listen to the voice of conscience and follow it, it will protect us by distinguishing between what is right and what is not. Our conscience and the work of the Holy Spirit in the life of a believer are not exactly the same, but they are similar. Just as our conscience guides us between good and bad, the Holy Spirit convicts the new man created in a believer when he does something that does not suit him and helps him to walk in the right way. He helps him but never forces the believer. In other words, every time the believer surrenders himself to the voice of the Holy Spirit, the voice of his conscience grows louder and louder, increasing his ability to make the right choice. It enables the Holy Spirit to continue sharing God's eternal thoughts.

Types of Consciousness

At least four types of conscience are mentioned in the Word of God:

- *Good conscience*—1 Timothy 1:19: this conscience pays attention to God's guidance, voice, and warning.

---

84 NKJV

- *Weak conscience*—1 Corinthians 8:7–8: this conscience is weak and prone to temptation, quick to accuse and condemn itself.

- *Impure conscience*—Titus 1:15: this conscience is corrupted by sin and cannot distinguish what is right from what is not.

- *Stunned or seared conscience*—1 Timothy 4:2: This conscience is inoperative because of its stupor. It happens because of repeated disobedience to the warning of the conscience and God's voice. This kind of conscience, as stated in Romans 1:21–24, states that those who have it are conscious that God has abandoned them because they are given over to themselves and sold to do evil. Because he is numb, he does not feel any regret or guilt when he does evil.

Romans 2:14–16[85] said:

For when Gentiles, who do not have the law, by nature do the things in the law, these, although not having the law, are a law to themselves, who show the work of the law written in their hearts, their conscience also bearing witness, and between themselves *their* thoughts accusing or else excusing *them*) in the day when God will judge the secrets of men by Jesus Christ, according to my gospel.

Beyond conscience, God had given the Jews through Moses the law to distinguish sin from righteousness, right from wrong. As a result, the Jews had a written law to refer to when they did something wrong. According to that law, the Jews distinguish between what is right and what is not.

But not so with the Gentiles. How can nations be judged before God without a law given to them? The apostle Paul gave an amazing answer to this great question. The answer is this. Although the Gentiles did not have a written law at their disposal like the Jews, they were given the gift of conscience. This conscience is not a law written on paper but a law written in the human mind. Not only did he write it down, but he included a balance in it so that they could consider this law in their minds as he wrote it down. He kept this balance as correct and true.

The law of conscience is not a written law that waits for a person to go and see it, but when he starts doing something outside of the law, it

---

85 NKJV

wakes him up like a bell that wakes him from sleep and tells him that he is out of balance. This is when a person uses his or her ability to choose. Although God has given this law to man in his conscience, for various reasons man violates the voice of conscience and that warning bell and enters into error; he will be saved by returning. The law of conscience is to raise its voice and not decide. But the electorate, which is one of the parts of the conscience, makes a rational decision.

Let's look at the verse that we saw above in Romans 2:16. The word hidden in the human heart or secret used in 1 Corinthians 4:5[86] is called motive. Our conscience is balanced. It has a voice. We said that it is not only a signal to distinguish what is right from what is not but also a bell that shouts that it is not right so that we do not make a mistake.

When a person lives on this earth, he is limited and imperfect in all things, so he can make mistakes when considering things based on personal needs and benefits or partisanship or seeking honor. It's not a mistake, but the motive has a deeper meaning than the action. It is surprising that man hears the voice of conscience, but only God knows the deep reason and gives judgment. This is why the apostle Paul said in 1 Corinthians 4:4,[87] "My conscience is clear, but that does not make me innocent. It is the Lord who judges me." When a person makes a decision based on his conscience, it may be right in his eyes; however, it can be wrong in the eyes of God.

This is because the reason behind our decision may seem right, but the motive behind our action may not be right. Only God knows that motive. The apostle Paul advises not to judge anyone before the time is right. The relevant passage is 1 Corinthians 4:5,[88] which states that we should "wait until the Lord comes, for He will both bring to light the [secret] things that are hidden in darkness and disclose the motives of the hearts."

This is like a white piece of paper or a clear glass. I mentioned earlier the idea of the virginity of the mind when the human consciousness is still being formed. Eve's conscience was pure and virgin until Satan came.

---

86 AMP
87 NIV
88 AMP

Spiritual Mind

As we have seen in the types of consciences stated above, conscience can be dull, weak, and dirty. However, apart from the salvation of our souls in the saving work of Christ Jesus, one of the great gifts given when a person believes in the Lord Jesus and is saved is a clean conscience.

In Hebrews 9:14, the great power of the blood of our Lord Jesus Christ was shown by purifying this dirty conscience. It is because He cleansed the conscience of a person who had violated the Lord's law for centuries and trampled on the voice of his conscience and lived in rebellion like a child, erasing the past and giving him the freedom to worship God. This power of the blood not only saves us but washes us, cleanses us, and sanctifies us so that we can come with a clean and blameless conscience whenever we come before God. In Hebrews 10:22[89] it states, "Let us draw near to God with a sincere heart and with the full assurance that faith brings, having our hearts sprinkled to cleanse us from a guilty conscience and having our bodies washed with pure water." The blood of Jesus Christ can cleanse us from the evil conscience.

Since this conscience is a reason-giving, selective, and decision-making part of us that is important, we should pay more attention to it and listen to it. Conscience is dangerous and can lead to death if its voice is not heard and it is drowned out by other voices. The problem for a driver who runs through a red light is not only that he did not obey the law but that one day he may be hit by another car or cause an accident. Violating the voice of conscience is the same, so knowing this, we should be careful before we cause danger to ourselves or others.

Even if they are Christians who have experienced salvation, they can use insults and hate to do evil and possibly make a brutal action like murder. Even as ministers, when they are used to living in violation of the voice of their conscience and the voice of the Holy Spirit, they may be perceived as speaking and acting no better than a godless person. The apostle Paul said that even as Christians, people can go against their conscience and harm themselves and others. In 1 Timothy 1:19,[90] he said, "Holding on to faith and a good conscience which some have rejected and so have suffered shipwreck with regard to the faith."

---

89 NIV
90 NIV

Being a Christian should not rob us of our conscience. Spirituality does not mean not using our mind; instead, we should train to think and choose according to God's Word by keeping clean while feeding and washing with God's Word. We are not conscience, but we have one. Our conscience is a great gift given to us to use, so we need to take care of and use it to keep it working properly. As the apostles cast away the things of conscience, when men cease to use conscience, they become like the helmsman at sea on a shipwrecked ship. This means being directionless people who don't know where to go and what to do and are capable of causing harm to other people beyond themselves. When we are aware of these, we should try to act morally at all times so that we can have fulfilling lives and be productive members of society and God's family.

Subconscious Mind

Our subconscious mind is completely different from our conscious mind. While our conscience gives reason, chooses, and decides things, our subconscious never gives reason, chooses, and decides. Our conscience is rational, but our subconscious is not. Our subconscious is lower than our consciousness. Since it does not give any reason by itself, all the information presented to it from our conscience is used in obedience.

While our conscience takes responsibility for our external body, our subconscious takes responsibility for our inner body. When we raise our hands, move our feet, speak, and eat, our bodies move only as we want or as our conscience allows. If this were not the case, life would be terrifying and shocking. It's like if our feet start walking without us knowing it or our mouth starts talking without our knowledge. This is why consciousness is given the power to control all of our external bodily movements. Any of our external organs are moved by the command of the conscience.

On the other hand, the conscious mind does not control the inner parts of the human body. Our heart does not beat when we command it, our stomach does not digest at our command, and our blood does not circulate at our command. Each of our internal organs moves according to the command of our subconscious mind, according to what God once programmed in our subconscious mind. Once created, they perform their work automatically without any conscious recognition or command from us.

Our subconscious mind does work beyond the inner parts of the human body. That is why some people call the subconscious mind the dark room. We cannot know what is going on in our subconscious mind. A photographer develops the film in a dark room. What he captures during the day, what we see, hear, and say throughout the day, develops the image of the day in our subconscious mind at night.

Our subconsciousness is the servant of our external body. I started riding a bike when I was a teenager. I was unable to adapt because of my fear of failure and my self-awareness. Surprisingly, I knew everything I was doing when I was still learning. I remember struggling to keep my balance as I held the handlebars and turned the pedals. This was my conscious effort to get used to riding. But after I got used to it, when to turn the pedals, how to hold the handlebars, and how to maintain my balance became natural. This is an example that highlights the difference between conscious and subconscious mind.

When I started to learn to ride my bike, I had it in my conscious mind. But after I got used to riding, I did it unconsciously. We are all like that. When we start something new, we are aware of everything that is going on in our mind. Once we get used to it, we do it without even knowing how or when we did it. As soon as I realized this, I tried to make changes in my life. I saw that by allowing my conscience to do something repeatedly, I was able to love what I didn't like and do what I wasn't able to do.

Washing the dishes after eating was one of the things I never wanted to do in my life. But eventually, as I grew accustomed to it, cleaning dishes was a simple task. I did it against my will, and it was never enjoyable. However, I forced myself to wash the dish I had eaten from, made a habit of doing so, and began to think about it repeatedly. Not washing dishes is now a tough thing.

This has had a great impact on my spiritual life. In the past, when I was facing spiritual problems, I used to fall in front of God in prayers and supplications and pray for the Lord to help me. Since the Lord taught me this, I never worry when my prayer life is taken away due to work, various problems, or the difficulty of praying again because the Lord gave me the key. I tell myself with joy repeatedly like this, *I can pray every day because ever since I received the Lord, the ability to pray is a part of who I am.* In addition, every night before I go to bed, I talk to myself, saying, *When I wake up in the morning, I will pray for a long time and will have a good time with my Lord. I am the son of God. It is my privilege to pray and to worship my God.* I go to bed meditating on Him, believing that the Lord has given me His grace to do this.

When I wake up in the morning, I have a strange desire to pray and wake with a pleasant prayer time. Sometimes I fail to pray for a day or two; however, I don't worry when I fail to pray because I know it's the thought I need to overcome. When I do this repeatedly every day, before I know it, I get back into that prayer habit I want.

In my view, our subconscious has two great functions. One is to control the human internal system created by God so that it works correctly without distortion. The second is to serve the human being according to the command that comes from his conscience. Every thought that is transferred to our subconscious by the will of our conscience will carry out the order given to it without examining and reasoning. A person takes the given information without choosing whether it is right or wrong, whether it is harmful or beneficial, and does a job similar to that information.

Our subconscious is like good soil. When we sow a seed of wheat or corn on good soil, the soil does not make a choice as to whether it is wheat or corn that I want, but it grows whatever we sow without question. The same seed multiplies and grows. In the same way, if a person thinks evil over and over again by choice of conscience, that person will undoubtedly be evil. Doing evil becomes the habit and the act of doing it without problem. That person's subconscious multiplies and magnifies that evil. Because of this, it makes it impossible to think, speak, and live without that evil.

If this person thinks about love again and again and deliberately stirs up his heart about love, just like good soil, his subconscious will multiply and grow love for him, and that person will not be able to think, speak, or live without love. Even in the face of those who hate and have done evil to him, he makes the response to be loving. He does this without any effort or fatigue. This is because the subconscious has the essence of love in it, so it cannot do or be outside of it.

During my ministry, I have seen quite a few people who are very good and who have God's great purpose become absorbed by the evil and false rumors they hear around them, and their goodness turns into evil. Not only this, but I have seen them being cruel, denying the truth, blindly judging, and being engulfed in evil.

I've seen people who spend time with wicked people and hear evil and gossip continuously. Without realizing it, evil is written on their subconscious, and they abandon their old selves, which is very tough to return to. What they heard and discussed without considering it or making a decision turned out to be a trap, and the seed they sowed via their subconscious is now strangling them back. I am amazed that once-loving people are now full of hatred and evil.

Our subconscious mind can grow and expand or crush and destroy all of our inner potential, according to the kind of seed we sow. All of us have been created with this gift by God. No one is created without a purpose and gift. One of the biggest differences between people is how we sow and what we sow in our subconscious mind. One is what our parents and our environment have planted in us, and the other is what we have planted ourselves by dealing with negative thoughts. Either way, any negative thought can be replaced with a positive thought. As I said, our subconscious is not selective, so if we tell our subconscious that we don't want the old seed, but what we want is God's Word in our conscience, by repeating this, we can remove that negative thought and change it with a positive or godly thought.

Anyone who has been told that they can't, they won't succeed, they're poor, they are not intellectual, they don't deserve education, they're not called, they're not anointed, the Lord is not with them, they can't pray, they don't understand the Bible has been touched by the problem of the seed in the subconscious. If that seed can be plucked out and another good seed be planted in it, there is no one who cannot change. I believe that if we think about what we want our purpose to be and say to ourselves the seeds that we sow in our subconscious—every one of our behaviors, all our bad habits—we can see a big change in less than a month. The problem is not to change the situation but to get out of that habitual way of thinking and change it to the right way of thinking. It's not the habit; it's the mindset we're used to that prevents us from thinking the good, but if we can think and change the mindset, it's easy to change.

This is one of the reasons why our internal emotions, such as fear, anxiety, and sadness, sometimes control us without us wanting them. Since our subconscious is also the seat of our memory and faith, whatever we deliberately put in our subconscious and accept as our faith prevents us from thinking and living outside of it, whether it is good or bad. This is why many people find it difficult to change their beliefs even when they know they are wrong. Since our belief is kept in our subconscious, it is possible to change our subconscious only by the command of our conscience. Of course, I said this in terms of human ability, but I cannot go on without mentioning that the Spirit of God can remove the evil influence of many ages in a minute. For there is nothing impossible for God.

PART THREE

Chapter 7—Mind and Knowledge

Proverbs 19:2,[91] "It is not good for the soul to be without knowledge."

Knowledge is the soul's nourishment. A soul without knowledge is hungry like a stomach that has not eaten bread. Hunger can only be satisfied when fed on knowledge. True knowledge is knowing ignorance. It is impossible to see the end of the horizon of knowledge but not the beginning. If our ignorance is not revealed when we come to know, it is doubtful that our knowledge is correct.

The Bible declares that knowledge puffs one up. He doesn't mean that knowledge is not needed when He says "puffs up," but He means that if ignorance does not make us humble and live in love, even knowledge will be useless to others and to ourselves. It is true that Albert Einstein said that knowledge could be acquired by any fool, but the point is to understand or comprehend because comprehension is what transforms information into knowledge. Knowledge is only available to those who seek it. Man's wealth is knowledge, but the poverty is ignorance.

The loss of the soul from knowledge is great. When knowledge is lost from the soul, a person loses the ability to reason. When he is unable to reason, he is less able to make the right choice. For this reason, he makes a decision based on the feeling he has in the moment or on the inspiration of other people and Satan.

In the verse we saw above, the amplified meaning of the idea that he who hastens his feet will stray from the path: "Also it is not good for a person to be without knowledge, and he who hurries with his feet [acting

---

91 NKJV

impulsively and proceeding without caution or analyzing the consequences] sins (misses the mark)."[92] The source of error and sin is ignorance. The beginning of wisdom is the fear of God. And to know the holy one is understanding. This is why the Lord Jesus said in Matthew 22:29,[93] "You are mistaken, not knowing the Scriptures nor the power of God." When He says that it is not good for the soul to be without knowledge, it is because ignorance and delusion are hand and glove. If there is ignorance, error or sin is inevitable. Hosea 4:6[94] says, "My people are destroyed for lack of knowledge. Because you have rejected Knowledge." The lack of knowledge mentioned in this passage addresses two lacks of spiritual knowledge. Although one is attached to the other by similarity, it speaks of both separately. The first speaks of God's ignorance of Himself, while the second speaks of lack of knowledge of the law, which expresses God's will, thoughts, and instructions.

As Israel is a kingdom of priests, it was God's will that we should know God's will as stated in the law and live by that instruction to be a sign to other nations as a teacher. However, when they stopped doing this, when they turned away from spiritual knowledge, their lack of knowledge resulted in destruction.

Ignorance and Destruction

A man of God used an example when he taught that ignorance is a destruction and the importance of knowledge. Smallpox was a devastating disease that claimed many lives in the world years ago. A person infected with this disease was certain to die. If he caught the disease, it meant death. Because of this, there was a great fear that many would not only be infected with the disease themselves, but their families would also be infected.

However, as soon as the cure for smallpox was discovered, this disease's power to kill and scare was broken. Today, people know that if they get smallpox, they can get rid of it by taking a vaccine. Not only the power of the disease to kill but also the power of fear has disappeared. Fear is overcome when knowledge comes. When knowledge comes, the

---

92 AMP
93 NKJV
94 NKJV

power of death is broken. He said, "Knowledge overturns the hardships brought by ignorance and brings freedom and courage." It's a wonderful example. If we see it spiritually, the example is true. The power of sin, disease, poverty, and many of our spiritual and physical problems has been broken by our Lord Christ Jesus just as the power of smallpox was broken when knowledge came. All the power of fear and anxiety, sin and death are broken. Two thousand years ago, the medicine was discovered, and a person can be saved by faith alone.

An unsaved person's problem is ignorance. The Lord Jesus, who is the answer to everything, finished doing everything on the cross and paid the price. Ignorance put the lives of many in prison and fear. As a result, many are deprived of the glorious life they should have. How many made an unworthy decision? This is why the gospel must be preached and the knowledge of salvation be proclaimed. When true knowledge comes, the free life of man is announced.

Colossians 1:9 says that for the people of Colossians, the apostle immediately prays for them to know the will of God after praising them for their salvation and for their perseverance in faith, their love, and the steadfastness of their hope. And if a saved soul cannot live knowing the perfect will of God, then its salvation will lose meaning, and it will begin to live a distorted and bitter life. A saved person's happiness and satisfaction in life are based on knowing and doing God's perfect will in his daily life.

Knowing God's will is like knowing the road map of life. Just as a person who starts a journey loses the direction of his journey, he loses the purpose of his journey and experiences a life of confusion, worry, and fatigue. This is what makes the lack of knowledge of the soul a disaster.

The apostle Paul also mentions two main things that are needed to know His will: spiritual wisdom and spiritual understanding. Spiritual wisdom is a matter of seeing life from God's point of view and living in fear of God. Knowing something and having a deep understanding of it are two different things. While spiritual wisdom gives us the vision, spiritual understanding gives us the understanding of that thing and the ability to use it properly. Without this spiritual understanding, the soul is lost and is like a confused captain.

Decision and Reasoning Skills

There is a journey of life between salvation and the end of salvation. It's important to live life every day. And life has balance. Depending on a man's decision, the balance tilts. And the soul is the seat of knowledge, emotion, and will. Will is the destination of our knowledge, and knowledge is the starting point of our decision. The knowledge we know determines the direction of our decisions and inclination. This is why it is said that knowledge is power. But the power of knowledge is the ability to guide people in the right direction. The power of knowledge ensures correct choice and decision making. When we say knowledge is power, we mean that it is reasoning power.

Discernment is the ability to distinguish evil from good, sin from righteousness, the noble from the disgraced, and the right from the wrong. Without knowledge, it is impossible to reason, choose, and distinguish. Will is individual. Neither men nor Satan nor even God can do anything until we decide. The good and bad things that happen in our lives are mostly thoughts that we have consciously or unconsciously dealt with decisions. It is our knowledge that controls our decisions.

Hebrews 5:14[95] says, "But solid food is for the [spiritually] mature, whose senses are trained by practice to distinguish between what is morally good and what is evil." Solid food is the word for righteousness. It is for people who have learned the spiritual doctrine and have accustomed themselves to live by that doctrine. These people can distinguish right from wrong. But what makes them discern is their knowledge.

A strong doctrine means a mature teaching of the entire Bible. This also shows the ability to know the correct spiritual teaching of the Bible. This is why when I mentioned the importance of reasoning, I stated that knowledge is the key. A person who does not sit down and learn the full knowledge of the Bible has little ability to reason. Because the knowledge that shapes the decision is less, not knowing makes him go astray in all his decisions and increases his ability to deceive others.

Accurate and complete knowledge is an indispensable issue for a person who wants to live a spiritual life. This is why the apostle Paul said

---

95 AMP

in Acts 20:27,[96] "For I did not shrink from declaring to you the whole purpose and plan of God." In another translation (NIV), he says, "I have not hesitated to proclaim to you the whole will of God."

What the apostle devoted himself to the Ephesian church day and night was to teach full spiritual knowledge. He taught them all the purpose and plan of God's counsel without leaving anything out. Among the biggest mistakes we see today is usually a lack of complete knowledge. When we say we know about something, our knowledge must be complete. Gathering information and knowledge are different. Indeed, the foundation of knowledge is information. However, knowledge is not just information.

Information is formless. Knowledge, however, clearly shows both ends. That is, it shows its shape and form. And if it has a structure, it makes the house of knowledge clearly visible and upright. When a person has full knowledge of Christian teachings, a house that is properly erected in the shape and form of his spiritual life will not be shaken by rain or flood.

When we learn correct knowledge in an orderly and proper manner, our ability to distinguish increases. One of the great abilities of spiritual knowledge is that it enables us to discern. People give in to wrong teachings and wrong actions because they do not have full spiritual knowledge, and their discernment is weak. Even the things that can be easily said wrong or right are readily misguided because they have not received the full teaching of the Word of God in a proper and orderly manner.

One of the biggest mistakes we see in modern times due to lack of knowledge is the issue of God's will. It is important to make sure that what a Christian intends to do is God's will or not. However, this is just one of the teachings of God's will, not the whole. God's will has at least three dimensions. One side is knowing His will, and the other side is knowing God's way. The third side is knowing God's timing. If God's will is not done in God's way and in God's time, a person who starts a path knowing only His will has lost his way.

By the will of God, the Israelites came out of the land of Egypt with wonders and miracles. There is no doubt that their going out was God's will. God has done many wonders and miracles to confirm His will. The

96 AMP

permit was issued, so why did they end up in the desert? If we look, the answer is in Hebrews 3:10–11,[97] "'They always go astray in their heart, and they have not known My ways.' So, I swore in My wrath, 'they shall not enter My rest.'" God's complete will was not only to take the people out of the land of Egypt but also to inherit Canaan. For this reason, God brought them out of Egypt in Deuteronomy 8:1–4,[98] "Man shall not live by bread alone; but man lives by every *word* that proceeds from the mouth of the Lord." The people who saw this great miracle did not know that they were guided not only by the will of God but by the ways of God also. God's will is not done without God's way. Because of this, we see the Lord swearing that they would not enter into His rest because they did not know the way (Hebrews 3:10–11).

God's will is done not only in God's way but also in God's time. This is why one of the ways that the people of Israel were led in the wilderness is by the cloud. When the cloud stops, they stop; when the cloud goes, they go. Time is of the essence. God had given Issachar's whole tribe the important task of discerning time and era. No matter how few, they were anointed for this work. Because God beautifies everything only in time.

I think that's why many believers and ministers are left on the road—because they don't know the way and the time of God. There are those who started in the spirit and ended in the flesh or started in strength and stopped in weakness. If they go out by the will of God and stay on the road, it means that they have either lost God's way or left before God's time. This is why not only knowledge but complete knowledge is needed.

In Exodus 19:4[99], we see, "Ye have seen what I did unto the Egyptians, and how I bare you on eagles' wings, and brought you unto myself." When He spoke about the purpose of their departure, He mentioned three things in verses 5–6, same chapter: (1) that they were peculiar and selected from the other nations, (2) that they were royal priesthood, and (3) that He had consecrated them for this work. This means that when God brought His people out of the land of Egypt, He chose them from among the people and sanctified them for His own work so that all other nations could proclaim and say that God is the only true God.

---

97 NKJV
98 NKJV
99 KJV

But they did not realize the reason why they were chosen and they were a holy people for God. Instead of announcing their God, they despised the purpose of being chosen by disrespecting other people. Because of this, the Lord has now brought an age of confusion to the Jews, sanctified and chosen the Gentiles in Christ, and called the king's people holy and a separate part of His inheritance. Thus, His main goal is to bring the Jews to Himself by making them jealous. What is surprising is that now the saved Gentiles have forgotten the reason of their purpose of calling. We see those who have been saved despise the unsaved who have been freed from demons and sin. They seem to look down on the unsaved, forgetting that the purpose for which they were saved was the reason for the salvation of others.

The Three Types of Knowledge

Three types of knowledge are described in God's Word. Informational knowledge, revelational knowledge, and experiential knowledge. The informational knowledge shapes our view of something through the information we get from the holy books and various teachers. The revelational knowledge is the knowledge that only God can reveal to us through His Spirit. Experiential knowledge is the type of knowledge that we know after we have verified whether it works or not by transforming the information we received at the level of information or revelation into action.

Spiritual Mind and Natural Knowledge

The Bible says that there is earthly and spiritual or heavenly knowledge. Earthly knowledge is all the information we take into our minds from the time we are born, seeing, tasting, touching, and hearing through our five senses. A person collects this information from his family, schools, books, movies, etc.

Just as there is natural knowledge, there is also spiritual knowledge. We get this spiritual knowledge mainly from the Word of God. True and correct spiritual knowledge can only be found when it is based on the Word of God. When a person holds these two knowledges in his mind, the Bible divides the human mind into two and separates them as the spiritual mind in Romans 8:6 and Ephesians 4:23 and the carnal mind in Romans 8:7 and 1 Corinthians 3:1–6.

What makes the human mind spiritual or carnal is the knowledge in it; there is no spiritual or carnal mind when it is created. The Bible calls a person who is guided by God's Word a spiritual person, and a person who is guided only by natural knowledge is called a natural person. After being saved, the person who is guided only by his natural knowledge is called a carnal person. Even if a carnal person accepts the Savior and is saved as a Christian, it is a carnal Christian that is not guided by the principles of God's Word in his daily life and has the same mindset as he was in the world. I call such people saved worldly. It is to say that they are saved and live according to the way of the world.

In 1 Corinthians 2:15[100] we read, "But he who is spiritual judges all things, yet he himself is rightly judged by no one." A spiritual person can know and examine both worlds, the spiritual and the natural world. When we go a little deeper in the verse, it explains that a natural person can only know and understand natural things. Spirituality is not just knowing only the spiritual knowledge. It is also when he develops spiritual thinking and applies his spiritual knowledge in his life; he can develop his knowledge of the natural world and use it for the glory of God by benefiting society.

The natural man can only know and understand the natural things. But a spiritual person has the ability to understand and examine both the natural and the spiritual. A believer is not based on knowing the Bible alone to be called spiritual. Basically, if we devote everything to the glory of God, all the work we do in the natural world is a manifestation of spirituality.

Daniel, Esther, and Zerubbabel did not sing and preach standing in the church or temple. But they made the name of their God known throughout the world. They melted the hearts of kings in their time. They made the people kneel to the Lord. They honored their God by living the spiritual principles they learned in their work responsibilities. Moreover, there are many who revealed spirituality through their intellectual work and research and glorified the name of their God.

---

100 KJV

In the world of science, we have seen a little of how much the natural mind of man has grown and what he has been able to do. This is a God-given ability to gather knowledge that is allowed to any person with a healthy mind and who devotes himself to knowledge. But with natural knowledge, it never makes him able to investigate and understand spiritual things. In fact, the more he is rich in worldly knowledge, the more he finds it difficult to accept spiritual knowledge.

Spiritual things are foolishness to the natural man. It cannot be understood because it can only be examined by the Spirit. But the spiritual man is able to prosper in natural knowledge and spiritual knowledge, and it is the main reason for the development of earthly knowledge. Christian scientists have made a great contribution to the world by contributing scientific discoveries, which are basic knowledge. Being spiritual does not preclude scientific research; rather, it is the source and justification for scientific research. When believers are spiritual, using their minds not only glorifies God's name but also contributes greatly to simplifying and helping the lives of human beings.

Spiritual Knowledge

Spiritual knowledge is divided into two parts: knowledge of information (logos) and knowledge of revelation (rhema). Each part is explained in more detail.

Knowledge of Information (Logos)

It is the knowledge of information (logos) that God has already given to man to guide him. Logos only gives us information. This knowledge not only allows us to understand God's thoughts but also informs us about His ways, His laws, and His plans. God told them to read it and to wear it like a bracelet on their hand, like a necklace around their neck, and stick it on their door so the Israelites would know that they should do this.

Any knowledge of revelation has its origin in the knowledge of the logos. God first gives the logos and then the rhema. Both are very important and are mutually dependent. Without logos, we cannot find rhema, and without rhema, logos does not give life. This is why we must first drink the Word of God like a child who is nursing milk. Then in the logos the Lord gives us rhema.

After accepting the Lord, a believer should first be interested in knowing the logos. Our thirst and desire to systematically know and learn the logos is our gateway to rhema because the origin of rhema is logos. If we see logos as a tail, we can see rhema as a match; it's easy to imagine what happens when the two meet. For those who say that they have a rhema that does not come from the logos, how do they maintain the rhema? And for those who only want the logos without a rhema, how do they ignite the logos? But the two together give a person a balanced and lasting life and service. Balanced spiritual knowledge should therefore be like this.

It is said that curiosity is the gateway to knowledge. Asking is the key to learning. While reading expands the horizon of knowledge, writing organizes knowledge. Finally, when we share our knowledge, we increase our knowledge. Our hunger to know the logos is like counting the first letter of the Word. When we begin to read the Word with this desire, our knowledge of the logos expands. When we put that down in writing, our knowledge begins to take shape. Then when we start sharing that knowledge with others, we start growing and multiplying in knowledge.

Knowledge of Revelation (Rhema)

The knowledge of revelation can be divided into three parts. We call the first revelation of salvation. This kind of knowledge is the revelation that is the light of the word that the Holy Spirit gives to people to understand the gospel they heard so that when they hear the gospel of salvation, they can accept the Lord and Savior. The second is the revelation of life. This is what enables the saved person to deeply understand the Lord who saved him and to understand the reason and main purpose of his salvation and to live the high-quality Christian life on earth. The third is called the revelation of greatness. This type of revelation leads to the sacrifice of the saved life beyond the normal life of the believer on earth. The experience is a type of revelation that is beyond the knowledge of the mind. It is important to explain these three in turn, so we will see as follows.

Revelation of salvation

In Matthew 16:17[101] we read, "Blessed [happy, spiritually secure, favored by God] are you, Simon son of Jonah, because flesh and blood

---

101 AMP

(mortal man) did not reveal this to you, but My Father who is in heaven." Then in Galatians 1:12,[102] the apostle Paul said, "I received it by revelation from Jesus Christ." The revelation that was revealed to Peter and to the apostle Paul was that Peter was among the apostles, and Paul was with those who were going to Damascus with him. Others heard and saw, but the revelation and the message came only to Paul. The revelation of salvation itself is the understanding that God gives to the believer. No one can understand the mystery of salvation either by education or intellectual knowledge. This is why when Jesus said to Peter, "My heavenly Father has revealed it to you," Paul said, "The Lord Jesus has revealed it to me."

The apostle Paul was a man who studied the law (logos) well under the feet of Gamaliel (Acts 22:3). In Philippians 3:8–9, he called the life and service that he lived only in the knowledge of the logos "a loss" before he received the revelation of Christ. In fact, considering that he had come between the true Lord and him and separated him because of the lack of education from this revelation, it made him consider everything he was doing in his life as garbage and rubbish.

On the other hand, he says that the spiritual knowledge that the Lord revealed to him on the road to Damascus led him to know Christ and the power of His resurrection until he wished to imitate Him in his death. The knowledge of logos made him persecute Christians out of zeal for the Lord, while the knowledge of rhema made the persecutor to be persecuted.

In Acts 23:6 Paul says that at noon suddenly a great light shined around him, which was the light of Christ, greater than the light of noon. When Paul met this light, he did not know the Lord whom he had served with zeal, so he asked, "Who are You?" This is a great sign that no matter how much knowledge we have of the logos, it will not lead us to the true salvation knowledge of the Lord.

Even today, though the light of salvation does not shine visibly on us like Paul, a great light shines on all of us who are saved. This is why the same Paul in 2 Corinthians 4:4[103] said, "Among them the god of this world [Satan] has blinded the minds of the unbelieving to prevent them

---

102 NIV
103 AMP

from seeing the illuminating light of the gospel of the glory of Christ." After saying that, in verse 6[104] he continues, "'Let light shine out of darkness,' is the One who has shone in our hearts to give us the Light of the knowledge of the glory and majesty of God [clearly revealed] in the face of Christ."

The difference is that the light that Paul shined on the inside was also visible on the outside, but the light of God's gospel has been lit in the hearts of all believers. This light shines the light of knowledge in our heart, the darkness of our heart's ignorance. That's when our story changed. Our life could not be the same. The truth dawned on us. We accepted rhema. This is the secret of salvation; God has removed the darkness of our hearts from death to life and from the kingdom of the devil to the kingdom of God. Hallelujah.

In the above two verses, light is associated with knowledge. The light of His glory's knowledge. Knowledge gives light. Ignorance is darkness. When the true knowledge of God is revealed to man, the darkness of man's ignorance is removed. Then human life and livelihood will begin to change. This is what we call the revelation of salvation, the light of knowledge that only God Himself reveals to people in His grace and wisdom.

The revelation of life

The revelation of life has two basic meanings in Greek. When a believer is saved, he receives the revelation of salvation. But after he is saved, he should find the revelation of life to live as a Christian and grow in the knowledge of Christ. This type of revelation is called an apocalypse. The meaning of the word is to reveal something that is covered or to reveal something that is unknown and hidden. In 2 Corinthians 4:3[105] it says, "But even if our gospel is [in some sense] hidden [behind a veil], it is hidden [only] to those who are perishing." Second Corinthians 3:15[106] continues with, "But to this day whenever Moses is reading, a veil [of blindness] lies over their heart." They are covered or blocked so that they do not see or hear. But for us who are saved, 1 John 5:20[107] states, "We

---

104 AMP
105 AMP
106 AMP
107 NIV

know also that the Son of God has come and has given us understanding, so that we may know him who is true." Everyone who knows the Lord is entitled to this kind of revelation.

He gave us the heart or understanding to know Him. The veil that covered Christ was torn from us. We now have the ability to understand Christ as we draw closer to Him. For a person who believes in this understanding, he will be able to live the true Christian life and serve the Lord by being rooted in Christ. Apocalypse is the highway to Christ. It is what strengthens the fellowship created between God and us and makes us see and live life through the lens of eternity when we live on earth. It is the knowledge through which we deeply understand the issue of our salvation.

To grow in this knowledge, we need the milk of the Word every day like a baby. Apocalypse is the knowledge by which we are strengthened in our Christianity by living a righteous life and distinguishing between good and evil. Apart from this knowledge, it is not possible to live Christianity with the knowledge of salvation alone. Just as once we are born in the flesh, we are not always born again, nor are we always born again in the Spirit. The revelation of salvation is the gateway to the spiritual world, not the main goal of our salvation. It is the beginning and not the conclusion of the great life to which we are called. This revelation of salvation helps us enter into the eternal and deep fellowship of our God. It is the door that the Lord Jesus opened for us so that we could grow in the knowledge of God and be able to live for Him and serve Him. Revelation of life is what helps us to be rooted in Him and build up by being before Him every day in prayer and His Word. It is the knowledge of revelation that is the never-ending school through which we grow from one revelation to another higher revelation.

The second kind of life revelation is known in the Greek word *photizo*. The meaning of the word is "to illuminate something." *Photizo* shows the expansion of the horizon of knowledge. The first revelation, *apokalupsis*, is to lift the cover, and the second revelation, *photizo*, is to turn on the light. The first one is to remove what prevents us from seeing, and the second one is to expand the horizon of our vision or give a deeper meaning by giving more light to the region of what we have seen.

Photizo is where we can see the Holy Spirit shining a light on what we see so that we can understand it more deeply. We see this in Ephesians 1:18[108]:

> And [I pray] that the eyes of your heart [the very center and core of your being] may be enlightened [flooded with light by the Holy Spirit], so that you will know and cherish the hope [the divine guarantee, the confident expectation] to which He has called you, the riches of His glorious inheritance in the saints (God's people).

We also see in 1 Corinthians 2:10,[109] "But God has revealed them to us through His Spirit. For the Spirit searches all things, yes, the deep things of God," and Proverbs 8:14,[110] "Counsel is mine and sound wisdom; I am understanding, power and strength are mine."

In the revelation knowledge world, the teacher and the revealer is God Himself. Isaiah 54:13[111] says, "All your children shall be taught by the Lord, and great shall be the peace of your children." In John 14:26[112] we read, "But the Helper, the Holy Spirit, whom the Father will send in My name, He will teach you all things, and bring to your remembrance all things that I said to you." God teaches in His Word. When the meaning of the word is enlightened, it makes all children wise. Linking the meaning of the word with light is that this revelation is not about opening the veil but about giving the light. In this light of revelation, we will find light to walk towards the goal of our salvation. This revelation is the knowledge by which we understand not only that Christ has saved us but also know who He is, His glory, His greatness, His power, and all His goodness. God is worshiped and served by spirit, and Christianity lives in the Spirit. While understanding the spiritual things and knowing the Lord Christ, we grow from knowledge to knowledge, not through the revelation of salvation but through the knowledge of the revelation of life. It is through this revelation of life that the church matures and separates from this world and becomes like Christ.

---

108 AMP
109 NKJV
110 AMP
111 NKJV
112 NKJV

All Christians and ministers should pray that this revelation will be abundant for the saints. Apart from this, if believers are not filled with the revelation of life after being saved and do not grow, they will become troublemakers by being carnal Christians. They will bring the world system to the church and try to compete with the world. When they try to understand and accomplish spiritual things through worldly philosophy, fatigue, and struggle abound, so their desire to live for the Lord and serve Him by surrendering to Him dies, and they become observers, not participators. Then they will move away from true worship. This is the beginning of all our modern churches' problem.

In my opinion, the church today does not lack knowledge. There are many spiritual books and schools. There are many colleges, universities, and Bible scholars. With the help of technology, a person can easily access many kinds of spiritual knowledge if he wants to. However, if all this knowledge of the logos does not bring us into the revelation of life, we cannot bring any change.

This revelation of life enlightenment is obtained first by humiliating oneself in front of the Lord and asking the Lord for revelation in prayer. Then it comes from studying the Word of God and meditating on it until we get the revelation. Next, it comes from having a true union with the Holy Spirit, who reveals all secrets.

No anointed Bible teacher or preacher can give revelation. All they can do is teach the logos. It is only the Holy Spirit who gives revelation. When believers have this revelation, they will grow in this revelation of Christ. Because of this, their mutual love, unity, and cooperation will increase. Our worship begins to be in truth and spirit. The world begins to see our change clearly and will glorify our Lord Jesus Christ. Then and only then will we be able to impact our world and be attracted to Christ for salvation.

The greatness of revelation

The greatness of revelation is the experience of those who have grown up in the second life of revelation and entered the depths of Christianity. In 2 Corinthians 12:7[113] it says, "Because of these surpassingly great

---

113 NIV

revelations. Therefore, in order to keep me from becoming conceited, I was given a thorn in my flesh, a messenger of Satan, to torment me." The greatness of revelation is the ultimate level of revelation as long as we are on this earth. This level of revelation allows us to experience higher spiritual truths beyond the natural world.

In the verse above, the apostle Paul says that the greatness of revelation is the kind of revelation where he went to the third heaven without knowing it in the body or without the body and heard unspeakable words, which are not lawful for a man to utter. In Numbers 12:5–8 it says that we have seen the life of Moses and that he was speaking with God face to face in the greatness of revelation. He also clearly stated the differences between the second and third revelations in the same section.

He says that he will reveal himself to the prophets in the second revelation of life through visions and dreams. But I will tell Moses (who entered the world of the third revelation) clearly, not by example but by saying that he will see God. The behavior of those who practice the spiritual life at this level is amazing. There was a time when they were separated from the natural world. This is why Paul said he could not tell whether he was in the body or without the body. When they walk at this level, they have two basic characteristics.

One characteristic is their great humble life. We see that even though the apostle Paul was walking in this greatness of revelation, he lived without telling anyone for fourteen years so that no one who sees or hears would consider him greater. Moses also did not tell anyone that he had seen God face to face until God Himself revealed it in chapter twelve. Above all, when God Himself testified about Moses, He publicly declared that he was the humblest person of all the people on earth.

But the second characteristic is their life of sacrifice. When the people of Israel worshiped the golden calf saying that these were the gods who brought them out of the land of Egypt, God said to Moses, "I may destroy them. Then I will make you into a great nation" (Exodus 32:10).[114] But Moses offered himself as a sacrifice, saying, "Please forgive their sin—but if not, then blot me out of the book you have written" (Exodus 32:32).[115]

---

114 NIV
115 NIV

When Moses asked God to erase him from the Book of Life, he did not miss what it meant to be erased from the Book of Life. But we see that the level of enlightened life that he had reached had brought him to such a great sacrifice.

When we look at the life of the apostle Paul, in the part of Romans 9:1–3,[116] he said:

> I AM speaking the truth in Christ. I am not lying; my conscience [enlightened and prompted] by the Holy Spirit bearing witness with me That I have bitter grief and incessant anguish in my heart. For I could wish that I myself were accursed and cut off and banished from Christ for the sake of my brethren and instead of them, my natural kinsmen and my fellow countrymen.

We see him preparing to sacrifice himself with great love and compassion for the Jews who stoned him and chased him from town to town to prevent him from speaking the gospel message. The apostle said that he did not do this suddenly and emotionally in one day. He described his sadness as a lot of bitter grief, but he called the time he was sad as continual sorrow or unceasing anguish. When he did this, he did it not with a wrong inner motive but with the testimony of the Holy Spirit. With all this, we can see that he announced that this life is possible.

Paul was a man caught up to the third heaven. I don't think he lost what it meant to be separated from Christ and to die forever. But we will see that this level of revelation prepares people for sacrifice as the height of the glory of his life reaches this point. True spirituality is loving those who hate us and not hating those who hate us. Like Jesus, not only does he love our enemies, but he is willing to sacrifice himself for our enemies. If a Christian or a minister begins to pray to reach this level, it means that he really understands the knowledge of the true Christian life.

This was the secret of Paul and Moses' life. Not to serve and become famous in front of people but to know Him and reach the greatness of revelation. Their prayers were not only for the success of the ministry, but their prayer was to know Him and to be like Him. As they lived to imitate Him, their ministry and influence were timeless.

---

116 AMPC

My main message in this chapter is that our daily decisions are crucial to our tomorrow. For our decision to be correct, we must have the right knowledge, both natural and spiritual. Where there is accurate and complete knowledge, we are empowered to live a productive life. Knowing that knowledge controls emotions and emotions will, we should grow up with knowledge and know that it is possible to live a life that honors God and benefits people in all our decisions.

Chapter 8—Mind and Emotion

Proverbs 15:13,[117] "A heart full of joy and goodness makes a cheerful face, but when a heart is full of sadness the spirit is crushed."

In English, there are two terms that have extremely similar meanings to the word "emotion." To start, I want to make it obvious which one I'm referring to by contrasting the two. Feeling is the name of the first emotion. This kind of feeling is the kind of feeling our mind experiences about our body. This feeling is a type of emotion that is a physical response expressed by our body. This is the feeling of hunger and fullness, and if it is on our external body, it is the feeling of cold or heat. These physical sensations are what our body wants or doesn't want through our consciousness, and it is a kind of message about our body that is transmitted by our mind. Either they are to protect us from danger, or, as hunger and satiety, they are feelings that send us to know our size or need.

The second type of feeling is called emotion. This feeling is what we feel intuitively or instinctively because of our reasons and knowledge. It is related to our beliefs, desires, thoughts, and actions. These are the emotions of happiness, sadness, anger, laughter, fear, courage, love, hate, etc. These types of emotions are expressed in our conscious and in our subconscious mind. What I want to mention a lot is this type of emotion because it is related to our spiritual and natural life.

Emotion and Science

Quantum physics researchers believe that every thought passes through our subconscious through quantum energy, electrochemical, and electromagnetic signals in our brain and body without our conscious awareness. For example, when we start thinking about someone we love,

---

117 AMP

the central part of the cells connects with our emotions and creates a pleasant feeling. At this time, the healthy feeling gives our mind and body a good attitude and strength to spend the day happily. On the negative side, that idea not only makes us weak by controlling our emotions and bodies but also has the power to bind us so that we cannot do anything in our spiritual or physical life.

Researchers believe that these non-physical light waves or energies shape our personality by 90–99 percent (Caroline Leaf, *Think, Learn, Succeed* [Baker Publishing, 2018], 39). These waves are the dominant reality and show how much we should be careful about what we think if the thought that shapes and controls our personality controls our emotions. Not being able to control what controls our personality, it is not difficult to imagine how negatively it controls our emotions daily. It is wise to think about how much it can change our day if we look at it positively.

The Inner Emotions and the External Body

The influence of a person's inner emotions on the outer personality is great. What goes on inside us is reflected in our outer self. It does not only reflect but also harms and benefits. A man's happiness is seen on his face. In Proverbs 15:13 it says if we see a radiant face, it is because of inner happiness. But with heartache, the soul is broken, or the inner spirit feels defeated. The reason a person lives in defeat is because of inner unhappiness or sadness.

Emotion is not a dream but a reality and is a part of our soul and a force that determines the success or failure of our outer life. Proverbs 15:15[118] states, "All the days of the afflicted are bad, but a glad heart has a continual feast [regardless of the circumstances]." Emotion can not only lighten and darken a person's face but also make a person's age bad and good. A person who is saddened inside has a worse time. He who keeps his inner happiness always makes his life full of joy, or it says that he lives a life of constant partying.

He who does not listen to his emotions will not experience life. The one who listens to his emotions and accepts them not only enjoys life but creates a sense of victory within and is motivated for anything and can

---

118 AMP

go beyond and influence others. It's also a contagious thing. If a person is seen laughing, soon everyone around them will laugh. If not, at least they smile. Similarly, when a person sits in front of someone who is crying, it is inevitable that they feel sad or cry. Just as being surrounded by sad people makes life sad, being around happy people makes us live a happy life.

Why Did God Give Us Feelings?

Emotions are one of the greatest gifts God has given to mankind. Emotion is one of the great things that separates man from other creatures. Today, science has developed mobile robots that can do many large tasks. They seem to think beyond the human mind and are reliable in their speed and accuracy. However, it is possible to give a correct answer based on the actions of any robot with the given information, but they have no life because they do not have a soul. Because they have no life, they have no feelings or emotions. They can neither love nor hate nor laugh nor cry. Just as God does not create anything without a purpose, when He places emotions in man, He does so with a purpose.

One of the reasons He gave emotions to humans is so that we know what we think. What's the point of thinking about love if there is no emotion of love? If we didn't have the emotion of hate, how would we know we thought about hate? When we think about something, it is one of the ways that we know that we are thinking, and it is an emotion that gives meaning to the thought that we have thought. We know what we think because we have knowledge. If there were no thoughts, we would not know emotion. For emotion is a reflection of our thoughts. What I think creates what I feel. Emotions cannot do anything on their own, so they need something to trigger them. In other words, emotions are a hindsight, not a forerunner. Emotions do not arise on their own without something to trigger them. When we know what we are thinking, we know why we have the emotion the way we do.

For example, if we put a snake in front of a twenty-year-old boy and a six-month-old child, the emotions of both are completely unrelated and different. But the difference is in their knowledge. A twenty-year-old boy knows what a snake can do if it bites him, and the emotion that comes from that knowledge is fear. But the six-month-old baby has no knowledge of what a snake can do to him, so he sees it as a toy and happily tries to hold it.

The unity between the two is that they both have an emotion on what they see, and what makes them different is their knowledge of what they see. The emotion created in both made one run away while the other drew them closer. The knowledge we have about life determines the type of emotions, and the type of emotions determines the type of our decisions and action.

A person who can create right and good emotions with the right knowledge will always have the ability to make right decisions. But a person who creates right emotions is only one who can think right things with right knowledge. Therefore, the growth measure of any Christian is based on what kind of intellectual lens they see the experience of life through and their ability to create emotions and the kind of emotions they create. God gave us emotions so that we know what is in our minds. Knowing that we only have to control what we think to control our emotions will protect us from problems caused by many mood swings.

A mature Christian knows five things about emotions. First, he knows what kind of emotions he feels, and second, he knows how to control and manage his emotions. Third, he understands the feelings of others, and fourth, he handles the feelings of others in the right way. Finally, he can think and live beyond his emotions.

Thought, Emotions, and the Spiritual World

Thoughts not only connect us to our body but also connect us to the spiritual world. Romans 8:6[119] states, "Now the mind of the flesh is death [both now and forever—because it pursues sin]; but the mind of the Spirit is life and peace [the spiritual well-being that comes from walking with God—both now and forever]." When we think about the Spirit, we find peace and life within ourselves. But when we think about the flesh, what we feel and face is death. And it makes us hostile to God. He says that thinking about the flesh is an enemy to God. Colossians

---

119 AMP

1:21[120] tells us, "You were far away from God at one time. You thought bad things and you did bad things. As a result, you were God's enemies." This shows that our thoughts are connected to the spiritual world. On the other hand, when human thoughts are spiritual and good, apart from pleasing us, they can also please God in the spiritual world.

In Genesis 6 verses 5–6,[121] it says, "The LORD saw that the wickedness (depravity) of man was great on the earth, and that every imagination or intent of the thoughts of his heart were only evil continually. The LORD regretted that He had made mankind on the earth, and He was [deeply] grieved in His heart." When our thoughts are evil, they not only make us sad but also cause sorrow in the spiritual world. This is why God saw the evil thoughts of man and felt sorry for him. Although God's sorrow and joy are not like human beings, it is certain that God has emotions and that He grieves and rejoices. Because of this, our thoughts are in contact with the spiritual world, so we see the ability to grieve the great God in this verse. We can see how much sorrow the human thought creates to make a world without sorrow.

Often the emphasis is on action. We care less when a man thinks evil than when he does evil. In the church and in society, the greatest fault lies not in action but in thought. Thought can dominate the human being by controlling the emotions. Our body is a reflection of our thoughts and a slave to our emotions. An idea makes an impact in the spiritual world before it is expressed in action. God knows and understands our inner thoughts, but Satan does not know our thoughts, so he reads us through our emotions, expressions, and actions. We have considered our words as actions. Because of this, they immediately respond to our thoughts and expression of feelings in the spirit world according to their identity.

Emotion and Human Connection

When we think about something repeatedly, we create an emotion, and that emotion becomes associated with who we are, and because of this, we may not be able to control the flow of thoughts in our minds. The freedom to think what we want at any time and in our own mind prevents us from thinking even the simplest things. It is at this time

120 EASY
121 AMP

that people begin to live a dull or unhappy life. Above we said that our thoughts are related to the spiritual world. As much as we allow the type of thought to influence us, it opens the door that connects us either with God or with the world of evil spirits.

We need to be especially careful when a close family member, father or mother, child or sibling dies because if we do not control our thoughts and think too much sadness in our hearts, we are more likely to invite the evil spirit world into our lives. About this matter, a man of God said, "Satan can stir up evil in people by creating evil thoughts. What is worse than this is that a person can wake up the sleeping devil by thinking evil thoughts over and over again." If people think negative thoughts repeatedly, they can become delusional. Moreover, Satan can use that negative thought of sorrow to make them live in isolation from people or even kill themselves.

Realizing that, we find it is necessary to be careful with our emotions so that the world of evil does not get a chance to give it power. Of course, it is appropriate and important to express our feelings to our bereaved families. If sadness does not find a channel to flow, it is worth knowing that it sits inside us and creates problems. Even the Lord Jesus wept knowing that He would resurrect Lazarus. Expressing emotions is normal. However, letting the feeling of sadness control our thoughts is like opening the door to the world of evil as mentioned above.

When we think about a thought repeatedly, we create a mindset. This attitude requires us to live a happy or sad life or to do something pleasant or unpleasant. And these actions go beyond us and create habits, behavior, and even culture for everyone who sees us. It is in this way that by growing from individual to family, from family to society, the face of our world is changing with evil and violence.

Spiritual Life and Emotions

The sons of Korah discussed the advantages of making the proper choice in Psalm 42:11[122] by speaking to the soul and managing emotions, "Why are you in despair, O my soul? Why have you become restless and disquieted within me? Hope in God and wait expectantly for Him, for

---

122 AMP

I shall yet praise Him, with the help of my countenance and my God." By generating the proper emotion with the help of the appropriate information, they talk to their soul to be joyful in a tragic circumstance. They instruct it on how to lead a moral life.

A thought can only be defeated by another better thought. We control our emotions by controlling our thoughts. Many times, when my thoughts troubled me, I would try to resist them by rebuking them and calling on the name of the Lord. The Lord's name is a great and powerful name that can defeat any enemy. If the thought I am thinking is from Satan and the evil behind it, I have seen it fall down. However, in the name of the Lord, I cannot oppose any of God's own thoughts or thoughts in my head or memories of bad times in life because I cannot resist the Lord or myself.

We overcome God's will only by saying yes to God. But we will overcome our own thoughts with another thought that is better and good and according to the Word of God. When we can do this, we can live a happy life by creating a happy emotion and being the controller and master of our emotions. I don't let my thoughts control me, but I control my thought, for I was not created to be controlled with thoughts but to think thoughts for my benefit. When I control my thoughts, I control my emotions. To change how I feel is to change what I think. For my thoughts are the stirrer of my emotions. A feeling is an internal movement that is motivated by a thought that arises from knowledge in my mind.

Sometimes when I can't think straight, I try to identify what I'm feeling at the time. If I'm feeling unwanted or anxious, I look back on my day and find out where the problem lies. I often find myself thinking that it will either be a bad word from someone or something that I want to avoid. Then, by changing that thought I don't want with the thought I do want, I will regain my happiness by changing the way I feel.

If I want to create a good emotion about something, I think about it by using the knowledge I have not only once but repeatedly and in different ways until I create that emotion in myself. This will not give Satan a chance to take my happiness because I've gotten used to that thought.

People become subject to their emotions without controlling them. When their emotions are bad, many of them feel sad, ashamed, and regretful. If we can't control our emotions, emotions will explode like explosives. If we cannot control our emotions, our emotions will inevitably control us because emotions are created by us. No one or nothing is the creator of good or bad emotions.

It is clear that things that are outside of our thoughts and hurt our emotions can arise. However, the lens through which we see those things determines the type of emotion that is created within us. If we allow all the problems from outside to make us sad, it becomes difficult to imagine where life will go and what we will become. This is why Solomon said, "Keep your heart with all your attention, for the concerns of life arise from it." For it is our heart that filters out what goes in.

Thoughts sometimes come to us knowingly, and sometimes they come from our subconscious without us knowing. All the thoughts we unconsciously put into our minds can one day create emotions we don't want without asking our permission. Not only can they create the emotions, but the speed with which they create the feeling magnifies the problem. Any information in our body moves at an amazing speed. Psychologists say that it takes only one hundred milliseconds for an emotion to form in our subconscious mind, but it takes six hundred milliseconds for our consciousness to register this emotion.

This means that before we decide that we don't want to be sad or upset, a look of frustration quickly appears on our face. Or before we even start thinking, our anger is expressed in five hundred milliseconds. Although our emotions manifest at this speed, they are not the activity of our mind that we cannot control.

Every human being was not created to be driven by emotion. In fact, we were created with a pure identity either by our family upbringing, society, or our bad experiences in life. We may be forced to hold unnecessary harmful emotions to rule us, but we can train our minds to create pleasant emotions by thinking good thoughts every day (Leaf 2018, 66).

As I tried to explain above, if we allow the unnecessary thoughts that have entered our consciousness to control us, they will control us until we cannot control their speed in any way. Our habit of putting the correct thought into our conscience is defined by the type of emotion and the speed of it. If we let our emotions take over, we lose control. If we control our thoughts for what we want, they serve us as our slaves.

In her book, Dr. Caroline Leaf tells the story of twenty-five years of research by Lisa Feldman Bret, an emotional expert, who states the billions of cells in our brains respond only to the direction we direct them. The cells of the body do not move by themselves, but they are guided by the will of our consciousness or our subconscious predilections. We are the leaders. They follow the direction of our thoughts and desires and shape our emotions (Leaf 2018.).

This shows that everyone has a natural ability to control and develop their emotions. When the sky is grey, we say it is about to rain. In the same way, we can see our emotions and talk about our mind's thoughts. The difference is that we can't control the clouds, so it rains. But because we can choose and control our thoughts, we can block the rain of emotions that is about to fall. The leader to our life steering wheel is in our hands. It is given to us to direct in the direction we want. But the problem is that when we let others take the lead of our life, it causes confusion and unnecessary cost to our life.

I've heard many spiritual people say, "Don't follow your emotions." I say that a person should always follow their emotions. When we know how we feel, we can know what we think. Of course, it is dangerous to follow emotions in order to be led by emotions. If we follow emotions to know our thoughts or to understand the internal problem that created the emotion, then following our emotions is a solution.

I have seen people struggling with their emotions and trying to overcome their feelings when they are hurt, but this is like trying to destroy the fruit without uprooting it. What matters is the thought that created the emotion. When we stop it or change it with another thought, our emotion will change according to our thoughts. A person who does not control his emotions by following and changing his thoughts will not be able to be happy or successful in life in any way because nothing he can begin will end. A person who does not control his emotions may hate the work that he started to do with joy and dedication today and stop doing it because of the emotions of tomorrow. The graph of the relationship between God and other people will constantly fluctuate up and down.

We are not responsible for every emotion we feel. But we should know that it is our job to control and manage our emotions. We must not allow our emotions to work against us but for us. If we look closely at the reasons for the success or failure of the people we see in the Word of God, one of the most important issues is whether or not they control their emotions.

Usually when Satan wants to direct our life in the direction he wants, he hurts our emotions by focusing on our weak side. A person who does not control his emotions or who cannot take responsibility and take it in the right way is always a victim of the enemy and will be used by the enemy.

In Genesis 4:1–9, Cain was very angry because God did not accept his sacrifice, and his face darkened. However, God advised him that this anger should not rule him, and he should keep the commandment given by God and reign over sin. But when Cain couldn't control his anger, he got the power to kill his own brother and became Satan's tool. Cain was angry before he killed Abel but not after he killed him. This negative emotion that was working against him got stronger with envy and forced him to be cruel to his own brother.

God had given him the opportunity to control and reign over the anger before his envy had conquered him. But his anger blinded him until he killed his brother. When his anger cools down, we see that he is very sorry. It is for this reason that God has marked him so that no one can kill him. If Cain had taken time to think while he was angry and had returned from his anger, he would have reigned over sin and not been a tool of Satan. He became a man who did not control his anger and did not turn back from doing what he regretted. Bad emotions rise like a spring water and flow like a flood, and if there is no stopping it, like a great tsunami, it will not return without causing much damage. But whoever stops the small start will be saved from the tsunami.

David, the psalmist, said that it was something that hurt the feelings of all the people in Ziklag until they lost the strength to cry. When his own army was raised against him, David took his thoughts away from the people and the things that hurt his feelings and raised his heart to the Lord, who gave him joy and hope. It was written to him, and David strengthened his heart with his God.

This is what it means to manage emotions. His own family and his entire army fell on the ground and choked with grief; his own army rose to stone him. On one hand sadness and, on the other hand, anger challenged him, but David strengthened his heart with his God. Because of this, David made the conclusion of this story one of joy and victory. He changed the bad emotion into a good one. Instead of thinking about the problem, he turned his heart to God, and the result brought him and his army and all their family back to great joy.

It is emotion that kept the great man of God, Moses, from seeing Canaan. Although he was jealous of God and was angry with the people of Israel, his anger prevented him from inheriting the promised land that he had been waiting for forty years by hitting the stone when God told him to speak. Moses' anger cost him until God Himself told him not to ask about this again.

Worse still, he instilled a sense of fear in his disciple Joshua, causing him to die late in life without producing a successor. Joshua warned Israel in the right way, and instead of making the people worship God, he saved himself by saying, "My house and I worship God, but you choose today what you will worship." This led to the coming of the age of Judges. Dealing with emotions appropriately, making decisions in rage, and holding back from doing things in fear all carry the same danger. When one person displeases God, the other person profits while harming the generation.

At various times in my life, when I am faced with life experiences that make me sad, I say to myself that I choose to live happily. I have seen this help me many times. Life is a matter of choice. Today like this and tomorrow like that. One like this and the other like that. As there are sad things in every day, there are also many happy things in the same day—sometimes through my own fault and sometimes through others.

Once upon a time, our church fell into such an unspeakable harm because of the problems that a few people raised. Because of this, the hearts of many saints were broken. Above all, those who were immature in the Lord were perplexed, and some have returned to the world from faith. Because of this, I felt great sadness and hatred for those who did this. The hatred that was stirred in me was not because of the damage to my personal life. When the hand of God was moving and the Lord was going to take the church to another level, they did this by disrupting the work of the Lord. Although I know that hatred and sadness are not from the Lord, the situation did disturb me.

At this time, I began to cry out to God from the bottom of my heart as my soul was being abused by a tsunami of hate and sadness, "Lord, I know that I cannot live in hate and sadness while serving You, so please save me from this tsunami of emotions." I begged Him to show me what to do. The Lord instructed me to do something difficult that seemed very simple. This is what He said to me, "Bless them every day by calling out the names of the people you call wrongdoers; bless them with everything that pleases you, and I will bless you."

Of course, I did not want to do this in my flesh, but I did not want my soul to live in this ocean of emotions. Moreover, I realized that if I wanted to worship the Lord in truth and spirit, I had no choice, so I began to pray for the help of the Lord's Spirit, calling their names in my prayers every morning and night. For the first few days, I felt like a person who has been nauseous after he eats something he didn't like. However, with the Lord's help, I abandoned my thoughts and the desire of my heart and was inclined to do what the Lord commanded me. In a strange way, after three days, I could feel my emotions of hatred for those people come out of me like vomiting.

What's more, that's when I started feeling love for these people. Unbeknownst to them, I hugged them and started kissing them. As I turned my thoughts and desires to blessing, my joy returned, and my love for the people was renewed. That evil emotion that came to destroy me left me. To this day, an amazing love was given to me for these people. Had it not been for this, I would not have had my ministry. A flood of emotions would have swept me away. When my resentment against the men aroused the emotion in me, the way to reverse it was not to resist that emotion but to do the opposite. When I changed the thought of hate to love, my hate disappeared. When I replaced the thoughts of sadness with blessings, my sadness turned to joy.

Everything in life cannot always be happy or sad. Life is like a buffet. Sometimes the good and the bad are all present at once, but it's up to each person to choose. For me, it's always my choice to be happy. Many individuals crave things that make others unhappy. It is the way of the wise and sensible to choose happiness over sadness.

As the Word of God says in Romans 8:28,[123] "We know that all things work together for good to those who love God." Since this is true, it cannot be denied that things that hurt our emotions for the time being end up making us happy. What we must not take away from our hearts is our inner heart's desire. If we hold fast to and keep the joy of our hearts, the time of victory and glory will come later. A person who manages his emotions in this way will not only be happy all the time but will always be a successful person because success goes beyond money. Living a healthy, peaceful, happy life is the destiny of a person who controls his emotions and knows that God always changes everything for good.

The main things that help us control our emotions:

1. Identifying what we think
2. Separating our feelings from ourselves
3. Not judging ourselves when we are emotional
4. Changing the thought that disappointed us with another better thought
5. Looking for people or things that make us laugh
6. Meditating on the Word of God
7. Rooting out the issue that caused the emotion we don't want

---

123 NKJV

Chapter 9—Mind and Will

Matthew 26:39,[124] "And after going a little farther, He fell face
down and prayed, saying, 'My Father, if it is possible
[that is, consistent with Your will], let this cup [a] pass from Me;
yet not as I will, but as You will.'"

Will and Free Choice

One of the greatest gifts that mankind has been given is will. Consent is a precious gift, but it is also a dangerous one. The danger is that will gives free choice. It gives us the freedom to do and not do what we want. Man's will can even choose to disobey God, the will-giver Himself. God gave us the will to carry out His will. The problem is that when we forget that we were created to live according to His will and we violate His will with our will, our violation of His good and perfect will puts us under the power of the enemy, who does not respect our will and forces us only according to his will.

Because man has a will, he has the choice to do or not to do the beautiful will of God. However, this great gift comes with responsibility. If we forget our responsibilities while exercising our rights, our irresponsible choices will force us to not even exercise our rights. This is why Ephesians 2:1–2[125] says:

And you [He made alive when you] were [spiritually] dead and separated from Him because of your transgressions and sins, in which you once walked. You were following the ways of this world [influenced by this present age], in accordance with the prince of the power of the air (Satan), the spirit who is now at work in the disobedient [the unbelieving, who fight against the purposes of God].

124 AMP
125 AMP

Our sin is what we do voluntarily. The free will we were given was to do God's will. But when we leave the goodwill of God and live as we will, we fall under the will of the prince who works in the air and does not respect our will. When our rights fail to meet our responsibilities, it takes us out of the world where we do what we want to do and puts us under the power of the enemy, who is forcing his will. Our will never makes us live as we choose. Our will was given to live willingly according to God's will, not to do as we please.

There is nothing on earth that God does not rule and control. However, one thing He does not control is the human will. He gave the power of the will and made man to rule himself. The problem is that when a man does not use the opportunity given to him and fails to submit his will to the One who gave His permission, the things that are ruled without his consent are placed on him without his knowledge, and the boss becomes a slave. No matter how noble a person's will is, if he decides to live as he wills without knowing why this permission was given, it makes him subject to the things he rules without his consent.

In Proverbs 23:7, it says, "As a man thinks so is he." The Hebrew translation of the word in his heart is not about our conscience but about our subconscious. Once we have chosen and kept every thought in our subconscious, it is He who directs our will. Our identity is in our sub-consciousness. Our subconscious overpowers the will of our conscience and controls us to do things we don't even want to do. Both our bad habits and the good ones have their source of power in our subconscious. If we think good things repeatedly in our conscience, the power of our subconscious will make us do good, and if we think bad things again and again, it will force us to do evil.

This is what we call addiction. Whether it's wasting money, insulting, gossiping, or lying, everything we do knowing that we shouldn't do it, we do it because of our subconscious mind. Everything that we think repeatedly in our conscious mind is imprinted in our subconscious mind. When the printed material comes out of the printing press, the way we look at life and our observation of life and the reality of life will be the same.

It is our subconscious mind that controls what we do, consciously or unconsciously. Once it is imprinted, we must deliberately think again and again about the idea we want to change and the idea we don't want. When we do this, we can overcome the habit or addiction that we don't want or uproot the thought. Focusing on something with our consciousness is the source of the power of action.

After people have accepted the wonderful mystery of salvation of our Lord Jesus Christ, they will be filled with the Holy Spirit and live for a long time subjected to many unwanted bad habits and addictions. As a result, they cannot experience the joy of salvation, so they live under accusations and attacks from the enemy. They lose the ability to do what they want to do. The big problem with this is that even though our spirit is saved, our soul is not yet saved. The salvation of the spirit is immediate, absolute, and requires no work except faith. But the salvation of the soul is slow, gradual, and requires our efforts. The effort is to change our thinking by the renewing of our mind.

Romans 12:2[126] states:

And do not be conformed to this world [any longer with its superficial values and customs], but be transformed and progressively changed [as you mature spiritually] by the renewing of your mind [focusing on godly values and ethical attitudes], so that you may prove [for yourselves] what the will of God is, that which is good and acceptable and perfect [in His plan and purpose for you].

The will of the world and the will of God are our daily invitations to live life. But it is our mind that determines which one we live, for the will is in the mind. In many of his letters, the apostle Paul commands his listeners to do what they should do in the Spirit. But in this section, he makes his plea for the mercy of God because it requires human consent. He not only begs but also raises the solution for them to know God's will and not live like the world. This means that they can only be transformed by the renewing of their mind.

Change is in the mind. There is no other option but to change the mind to overcome any life habits that we bring from the world that do not honor the Lord and to live the victorious Christian life. If there was another option, the apostle would have written our choice. Since there is

126 AMP

no other option, he invites us to change our minds with the knowledge of God's will. The reason why there is no other option is that change requires human consent.

Real change starts with a change in thinking. Renewing the mind means changing the way you think. It is changing the world's thinking with spiritual and biblical thinking. There is worldly thinking. There is also spiritual and biblical thinking for Christians. Our thoughts determine what we look like. This is why he advised not to conform to the world—because change is related to the mindset. No one has changed his life without changing his thinking. The source of godliness comes from thinking according to the Word. God's will is to know what is good, acceptable, and perfect. To do God's will, we have to know God's will and change our mentality according to His will.

The Will of God and Man

The knowledge, emotions, and will of the human soul are the essence of life. Of these, it is the will that determines the direction and destination of our lives through the influence of knowledge and emotions. Just as a parent would be happy to do everything for his child, God is a God who enjoys doing things for us and our happiness. God is a good and merciful God. The problem is not God's will but God's inability to do anything without human will.

If He gives us something we don't will and don't want, it's a violation of our will. If He violates our will, human life will be like an animal and an inanimate creature, and because of this, when He wants to do anything, He waits until we give Him our permission, for He can do nothing without our consent. Since God taught me from His Word that He would not bless me without my consent, I have noticed that I must first give my consent to everything I ask from the Lord by making sure that I want it from my heart.

The main reason I do this is because I understand that He can't give me something I don't want without my consent. If He gives it to me without my permission, it violates the will He gave me. This is why Jesus Christ asked the blind Bartimaeus, "What do you want?" It may seem like a strange question to ask a blind man what he wants, but for the

Lord, if the blind man opened his eyes without wanting to, that would be a violation of his will, so He had to wait until the blind man himself said he wanted to see.

Genesis 2:18 tells us that God intended to give Adam a wife. However, in verse 19, instead of giving him what He intended to give, we see Adam bringing animals and naming them. When Adam was sorting the animals to come up with names, he noticed that all the animals were male and female. For this reason, it says in verse 20,[127] "But for Adam there was not found a help meet for him." If we say that someone did not find it, it is obvious that he was looking for it.

After seeing Adam's desire, we see God bringing Eve to him. Adam's desire shows his will. When Adam wanted, the Lord did what he wanted and allowed and brought her. And when Adam saw Eve, he said, "This is bone of my bone, and flesh of my flesh" (Genesis 2:23).[128] It was because God saw what Adam thought and desired in his heart. The Lord could not bless Adam with a wife without Adam's will and desire. God's wisdom is to help Adam by bringing animals to have a desire, and after seeing a desire in Adam, he gives Eve to Adam according to his desire.

Even today, God's way of working is the same. The Lord Jesus Christ did not force anyone even after He had finished working for our salvation through great suffering. Rather, He asks for the will of man, saying, "If anyone desires to come after Me, let him deny himself, and take up his cross, and follow Me" (Matthew 16:24).[129] The will of man is very noble in God's eyes, and He does not want to violate it. But when He sees the will of man, He rises to work. Philippians 2:13[130] says, "For it is [not your strength, but it is] God who is effectively at work in you, both to will and to work [that is, strengthening, energizing, and creating in you] the longing and the ability to fulfill your purpose] for His good pleasure." When heaven intends to do something, the Lord puts a will and desire in man; when desire supports will, the Lord gives us the ability to do that will.

---

127 KJV
128 KJV
129 NKJV
130 AMP

When we see the great turmoil that the Lord Jesus Christ was in at Gethsemane, the greatest struggle was the struggle to subdue the will. He was struggling with the choice of doing His own will or His Father's will. He did sweat blood to make a choice between His Father and His will. But once He made up His mind, He was able to drink the cup of the cross.

The problem of man is until he decides he can do it. After the Lord Jesus decided, He did not hesitate to give His life on the cross. The source of His power was that He first submitted His will at Gethsemane when He said to forgive them because they did not know what they were doing. His sacrifice was voluntary and not forced.

God cannot do without our will in the same way Satan cannot do without getting our will. He who has obtained our will has taken hold of us. Destiny is made by God. But we bring it to fulfillment by us who have the will in our hands. All a parent can do for their child is to get an education and pay the school fees. It is the will and decision of the child to study and get good results. This is what the Lord has done for us. He gave us everything we needed.

He writes the book of our lives, places gifts and talents within us, and prepares chances and opportunities for us. It is the homework of all of us to bring that chance and opportunity to its end by giving our will and working hard. Man can only give his will to God. What God does not have is our will. If a person withholds his consent and tries to give Him something else, he has no favor in the eyes of the Lord because we cannot please Him with something that belongs to Him. For there is nothing else that God does not have. We can please Him only by our will, which is not in His hands. For a gift to which our will is not bound is not a gift.

This is how the Lord Jesus pleased His Father. He started by saying that He had come to do His will and ended by giving His will. Man's success lies in doing the Lord's will. To do His will requires self-denial. Happiness is when we give up not only ourselves but our will. When our will is submitted to His will and our pleasure is in His choice, then we can please not only God but ourselves and others also.

This is the great mystery of Christianity. True happiness is satisfied by surrendering one's will to the giver of will. True worship is no different than surrendering one's will. Romans 12:1–2 talks about what true worship means. This is the plea of the apostle Paul. The body that we willingly gave as a living and holy sacrifice is called true worship. That is why it is needed to renew our mind.

A renewed mind submits its will to the giver of will, while the unrenewed mind forgets the One who gave it permission and lives for his will. God's will is good, acceptable, and perfect. "Be not conformed to this world" (Romans 12:2)[131] means to stop living according to one's own will. The satisfaction in the worship of the believer is subject to submitting his will to the One who gave his permission, right, and free choice of the will.

In chapters 7, 8, and 9, we tried to see a little bit of knowledge, emotion, and will, which are the main parts of the soul. If a believer understands the nature and operation of these three things, if he is able to have correct knowledge and make a right decision by creating good emotion, he is able to renew his mind. With spiritual knowledge, a person who can create spiritual feelings and make the right spiritual decision will be happy and successful throughout life and will please God and be a blessing to the next generation.

---

131 NKJV

PART FOUR

Chapter 10—Mind and Thought

Proverbs 4:23,[132] "Keep your heart with all diligence, For out of it spring the issues of life."

In this era, it seems that due to the chaos of the outside world, everyone has forgotten the inner world and has completely failed to connect with himself. Everyone seems to be at odds with themselves or afraid of themselves, so they don't have time for themselves. This prevents people from thinking. Although the civilization of the world is beneficial in many ways, it can also cause harm. In the civilized world as well as in the developing countries, technology has attracted people's attention and stolen society's alone time. Mobile phones, iPads, games, and movies have not only interfered with the person but also between husband and wife and children and have ruined and sometimes destroyed the time to talk and bond with each other.

Modern technology has made people look neither outward nor inward. It has prevented them from having time with themselves. As a result, it has blocked the flow of life from the inside to the outside. Life should flow from the inside out. A life based solely on external information without time for internal reflection is more harmful than beneficial. For life begins with rest, not running. A rested person is able to see within, but looking inside requires time to think.

Proverbs 4:24 reminds us that it is our heart or our thoughts that we must guard. The reason for this is that out of it are the issues of life. It's our inner thoughts that shape who we are and not what's on the outside. This verse clearly states a very important basic idea of life. The life in our heart is not only within us, but it is also the outlet of life. The imagina-

132 NKJV

tion created by our thoughts is revealed in our words and actions. What I think determines the nature and direction of life. Solomon, the wise man, reminds us that no one is held responsible for the losses and failures that have happened to us in life. Except for a few things, everything that happens in our lives is our own responsibility. Even if bad and unwanted things happen to us, we can change and overcome the external influence by changing our inner thoughts.

Thought and Mind

Thought is the inner world of man. Our perception of the outside world is like the inside world. Our outer world reflects our inner awareness. A person's speech and actions are according to his inner self. We express our thoughts through our words or actions, but we cannot express what is not in our thoughts through our words or actions. A person's inside world either beautifies or destroys the outside world. When we beautify the inside, we beautify the outside; when we spoil the inside, the outside is spoiled. A person who does not change the inside cannot change the outside. He who can change the inside can easily change the outside. We give meaning or reason to anything in life according to our thinking. Our thinking is based on our knowledge or the type of information we have internalized. We can build or tear down according to our thought or mindset.

We are all prisoners of our thoughts. Our perspective and horizon of life are like our thoughts. Some are prisoners of fear, hatred, resentment, sadness, bitterness, impossibility, love, peace, and happiness. The beginning of a freed man's freedom is the inner thought. Freedom is the inner world. No one can bind a person who is free inside. There is no doctor who can untie a person who is bound inside. It is not difficult to imagine who is in prison when the apostle Paul said to those outside of prison, "Rejoice in the Lord always." A person who is in prison with freedom inside says rejoice to the prisoners of thought outside. This is a significant proof that the freedom or the prison is within the man.

If our freedom, happiness, and success of life are based on our inner thoughts, then everyone should build his life with the thoughts that are the main driver of his inner world. In order to build a thought, it is necessary to think deliberately. Not thinking when we are concerned about something but thinking intentionally and deliberately before anything happens. It is not our experiences that concern us but the premise by which we see a precept that weighs, guides, and manages our experiences.

Everything Starts with an Idea

The Bible says that as a man thinks, so is he. If man is as he thinks, then we are what we think. Our body is formed by the type of food we eat; our inner self is formed by the type of thoughts we think and the time we give to think. When we know and shape what we think, we shape and know who we are. No one has more life than they think, for the human being is determined by his thoughts.

One of the greatest gifts that God has given to the human mind is the ability to think and meditate. Many people think that their thoughts are unrealistic and unattainable. But thought is a great force that controls all the movements of our mind and body as well as our emotions. Scientists say that every thought we think every day instantly affects seventy-five to one hundred trillion cells in our body. If this is true, then our thoughts control our whole being. It means that he who does not control his thoughts does not control his mind or his flesh.

Thought determines the kind of life we live, whether it is good or bad. Our life is like our thoughts. If our thoughts are good, our life will be good, but if our thought is bad, our life will be bad. Not only thinking good thoughts but hanging out with good-thinking people will change our lives. If people are surrounded by positive thoughts, their mental structure will change, which will increase their intelligence.

Thoughts can be triggered first by the things that we encounter from the outside world. Thought can also be triggered with the ideas that we have received and dealt with since childhood that are recorded in our memory. Scientists say that five to seven memories are sent to our consciousness every few minutes. So, if these memories are negative, then it is unquestionable that they hinder our daily life. It is not difficult to imagine that if every few minutes, there are thoughts that we don't want that can hurt our feelings, how much will they unnecessarily crowd us and disturb our life? (Leaf 2018, 210).

The solution to get rid of these thoughts is to be able to discern and choose the thoughts that we think every day, no matter where they come from. Our mind builds itself by gathering information, so what it builds and works on is the type of information. When thoughts come that we don't want and that can take our emotions in an unwanted direction, we should identify them and take them in the direction we want. Otherwise, a mind built with wrong information will lead to a wrong and unpleasant life. All the thoughts that we pay attention to and think repeatedly will not only stay in our minds for a long time but will become the beliefs that will determine our future choices. Every thought that we think of repeatedly has the potential to grow within us and control our life.

Depending on our upbringing, many of our thoughts may have been corrupted since childhood. However, we can change these thoughts. First, we need to identify these negative thoughts for what they are. It is very important to write down the thoughts that come and disturb us from time to time even if we cannot think of them all at once. After identifying the unwanted thoughts, the next task is to replace these negative thoughts with positive ones. A mind can only be changed by another thought. We should confess it to ourselves every day, out loud or softly, by deliberately and intentionally thinking about the good things that are opposite to the negative thought that we want. When we do this, we should not think that it is yet to happen and that we have to struggle to reach that thought. It is very important to think that through believing we can create thoughts that we want by focusing our thoughts on the present.

It is true that bad thoughts pass through the human mind without permission. It is not a problem that bad thoughts pass through us. The problem is when we allow these negative thoughts to take hold and control us. We can't stop birds from flying over us, but we can stop them from sitting on us and making nests. We can't stop all the thoughts that pass through our minds from coming, but we can stop them from sitting inside us. Before we accept and deal with a thought, it is very important to see and examine the thought carefully and see it as a way to solve the complex problems of life.

We have to take time and try to change the negative thoughts inside us. Studies show that the time it takes us to do this is at least twenty-one days. Realizing this, thinking about the idea we want, creating positive or spiritual emotions around the idea we want, and changing our focus, we can change our lives in just twenty-one days. Just as a hen sitting on her egg for a certain period of the day can hatch her chicks on the twenty-first day, if a person then, like the hen, deliberately sits on an idea for a certain period of time, a day can bring his thought into reality. Moreover, just as a hen can lay many eggs at once, a person can conceive and give birth to ideas by thinking of different ideas at the same time.

Thought respects what it respects and despises what it despises. If we embrace it, it will give us fruit; if we forget it, it will remain in the air. Our minds are designed to think. Thinking is the main function of the mind. When we remove that, it will be lazy. But if we think about it every day, it shows its ability. Although thought is an inner world that cannot be seen with the outer eyes, there is no one who cannot think. Everything we do every day, from the time we wake up to the time we go to bed, is driven by a thought. There is nothing we do without thinking; we think either consciously or unconsciously.

If there is a once-established habit in our mind, life will become repetitive, boring, and tasteless. If there are many corrupt and wrong thoughts in us, life will repeat mistakes and make it like going from Kadesh to Kadesh. Living in the same place, seeing the same thing, doing the same thing for forty years without change makes life meaningless. As I tried to mention above, the life of many people is like a car where the driver sits in front of life but gives the steering wheel to someone else. It is not enough to control the speed of the car but also the direction.

For those who make thinking a habit, who understand that thinking is their inner power and always meditate on quality and high thoughts, life offers its wide feast invitation with miracles. A feast is delicious, and it is suitable and pleasant for the natural and spiritual world. It is preferable to think than not to think; therefore, whenever we think, let us think about high-quality thoughts. Let thinking and meditation be the experience of our life. Just as an athlete's daily practice makes his muscles grow and become stronger, if we start practicing and training our mind to think with small ideas every day, we will have the ability to think and do even the things that are thought to be impossible.

The biggest problem in life is not action. If action gets the power of thought, it has the potential to do anything. The problem is not doing it or not being able to do it; the problem is the lack of power of thought. Everything that is said to be impossible is possible. Our talent and potential get their fuel from thought. I feel compelled to mention this after witnessing many people's and my own personal experiences.

I saw a man without two hands playing the guitar with his toes playing all four notes of music. I saw a painter who had lost both hands holding a pencil in her teeth and drawing as she used to draw. I saw others throw spears with their feet and hit a target. What do you call this? When a person with two hands cannot draw, others without hands draw with their teeth. When a man with ten fingers struggles to play the guitar while another without hands plays with his feet, what more evidence can there be that the greatest power in life is not from the outside but from the power of mind and thought?

I see a lot of people having a hard time doing or changing small things. I have heard them say that after many attempts they have given up. It is not that they can't but that they don't internalize the ability by thinking about it daily in their mental world. The hard part of life is to sit down and think every day. I don't struggle when I want to change anything, but I decide when and where to sit and think. I push what I think to go in the direction I want by being in the spirit of prayer and quoting the Word of God. When I think, I can imagine and visualize what I was looking for. Every day I meditate for a few minutes and wait for the feeling of happiness to arise. When I do this, I don't think anxiously because I want the thing to happen, but rather I think calmly that the thing will happen and that it will be revealed in time.

After a few days, I'll know when I feel excited about it and can do or be. When I understand that I have the power to do what I want, I will slowly train my body for the action of that thing. Strangely enough, I don't know how, but I see myself doing it, or I see it miraculously happen. For power lies in our inner thoughts, not in our actions. Sometimes I find it difficult to think about what I want when I can't see the way and the time seems too long. However, I stand thousands of miles away from any ideas of how and when. I know that God has the ability to do anything, and I have seen many things happen quickly when I surrender the timing to the Lord.

Thought and Flow of Thought

Thought is a mental activity or process that helps a person correctly shape the world in which they live their life plan, goals, and needs and interact with the world they live in. Thinking is the ability to understand the information in the mind, solve problems, and make decisions by giving reasons. Scientists say that more than 60,000 thoughts pass through a person's mind every day. As I tried to point out earlier, every thought we think every day instantly affects seventy-five to one hundred trillion cells in our body (Leaf 2018, 67).

That is why it is important to maintain a flow of thoughts in order to think. Being able to think every day for a few minutes without interruption or distraction brings inner strength. We cannot gain understanding until our thoughts take shape and form an image. If people say they don't understand, that means the picture has not yet taken shape. As soon as the picture ends, we say that we understand. This is the benefit of thinking.

Being able to think for longer periods of time throughout the day without getting distracted is a life-changing experience. This is one of the questions I ask when I teach in many places about the renewal of the mind. How many minutes in a day can you think without your thoughts becoming scattered or interrupted? Surprisingly, I have observed that not even one in a hundred can do this. This shows that our society does not have the experience to sit down and think, so when we say or do, we decide what we feel at the moment, not what we have deliberated or premeditated.

For this reason, whether we love, hate, oppose, or support, there is no good reason. What we think, oppose, or support is based only on the feeling of the moment. This is a big problem not only outside but also in the church. In order to think, we must first practice thinking logically without interrupting the flow of thought. When we do this, it makes us capable people who have reasons for what we do and what we say and who are not constantly changed by circumstances. This is maturity, and this is mastery.

Flow of Thoughts and Creative Ideas

From the flow of thoughts, books are written, pictures are drawn, music is composed, and creative ideas emerge. The greatest skill of any painter, musician, scientist, or preacher is their ability to handle the flow of ideas. There are people in the world who are considered great thinkers. All of them are famous people who have done great work. For example, Isaac Newton, Albert Einstein, Plato, and Aristotle are just a few to mention. Many great men and women of God can also be quoted from the Word of God. Joshua's victory is not only about his strategy and battle but for his victory and that he thinks about the Word of God every day and night. This is why it is said that if you think about it day and night, then you will make your way prosperous and you will be successful.

The secret of people with speaking skills is their ability to keep their thoughts flowing without interruption. When people begin to speak but are unable to say what they want to say because their thoughts are interrupted, the reason is that they do not have a flow of ideas or structured knowledge in their minds. The flow of thought is the ability to think without interruption of the processed knowledge in our mind.

A person who cannot inspire his spirit in any world of art cannot write or draw anything or come up with a new idea. Inspiration means when an idea comes down without inhibition and brings a new idea to us. All of us occasionally have a new and interesting flow of ideas that come to us suddenly. One of the differences between people is that one respects an idea and gives time to reflect and record the flow of thought, while one doesn't respect ideas and is able to ignore the time to reflect and record the flow of thought.

If we learn to wait and take care of this kind of flow of thoughts when it comes to our mind, our mind will learn to handle the flow. When our mind can maintain the flow of thoughts, it becomes easier to express the thoughts correctly and to speak or write and make other new creations. This flow of thought comes from practicing intentional thinking. This can be triggered when people give time to think by looking for things or places that stimulate their spirits and make them think without problems.

Protecting the Flow of Thought

Just as there are things that awaken our spirit, there are also things that destroy it. These include being around negative people, listening to music we don't like, looking at colors we don't like, being in an environment with a smell we don't like, or sitting in a cramped room for a long time. On the other hand, there are things and situations that trigger the flow of thoughts. This is available for everyone, although inner needs may vary. When Albert Einstein did not collect ideas while doing the work of scientific invention and lost the flow of thoughts, he said, "I play the violin and immediately I see new ideas springing up in my mind."

In my practice, when I listen to uplifting and positive discussions and conversations, when I read books that have a flow of thoughts and go with the grace that is within me, and when I listen to spiritual teachings, I know that the source of ideas opens up from within me. But often, when I want to think on purpose, I either drive a car or start praying. The places where I have made many of the biggest decisions in my life are in my car and my prayer place. I don't know why, but thinking in these two places makes my mind happy, like a person who enjoys eating food.

For some people, being by the water and listening to music lifts their spirits. For me, I can never think when I listen to music because I am amazed by the quality and creativity of the music, and I want my full attention to be in the music. If we know and grow in this way, we can be an influential person. Human greatness begins with deliberate thinking and increasing the flow of thought. It depends also on the quality, type, and scope of the area of thought.

Inspiration and Flow of Thought

God is the God who gives the inspiration of the Spirit. I often have this experience when preparing my messages. I know when ideas come to me that I have never thought of or heard of before. Like a person watching a movie, I see knowledge coming into order and form. When I wrote my first book, *Marriage and Secrets of Marriage*, I remember writing thirty pages in one breath in one night. This is the result of God's inspiration of our spirit.

Sometimes when I pray, I ask the Holy Spirit to help me not let these thoughts escape me because when these ideas come to me, they come to me quickly. Before I finish writing one idea, many others are arranged. I see the ideas lined up like an object. If they come in such a form, they often come in the form of images, so I do not forget them. Some of my messages have come to me in this type of method. Not when I was doing any research or reading my Bible but suddenly. Not only do I get the idea of the message, but I also get it in the shape of a vessel descending in a vision just like Peter did. From the beginning to the conclusion, all thoughts are maintained in the form of images.

At other times, I've seen ideas that come together over a period of a week to a month before it becomes a message. Sometimes, for more than a year, the idea is interrupted in different times and circumstances, but it stays like a fire inside me that will not go away, and when it comes, it is a big message. Although these are messages I will never forget, writing is a great memory tool, so I immediately write them down on my phone whenever the ideas come to me. I know that I have missed many moments that I will regret later in my life. Because of this, even if I'm driving, I'll record the idea on my phone, or I'll pull over and write it down. The thing that I never lose is a pen and paper or a recorder to record my thoughts.

We need three things to have a flow of ideas:

- An inspirational place
- A time to think
- A purpose and goal of what we think

If we go back and forth, in order to think about an effective idea, it is necessary to know and decide what we want to think about. This gives direction to the flow of our thoughts and lets us know when we are done thinking. When we think about something with a purpose, when we finish thinking about it, we are satisfied like a person who has completed a job. Because the end of an idea is an action, every idea that does not focus on turning into action is a waste of time. If we know the purpose of our thinking, we must decide the time of thinking. In this fast-paced world, if we don't set aside time and take the time to think about our work responsibilities, we will regret it when we get older.

Location is critical. The Lord Jesus usually prayed in the mountains or garden place. Sometimes I wonder why the mountains. Why a garden? I wonder if that is one of the reasons why the Lord prayed all night. Prayer requires thinking. Prayer is a place where we make many decisions and decide to put aside our own will to do the Lord's will. I see that thinking right and being in the right place to think are two sides of the same coin.

Many times, we may not have enough time to think about what we want to think. But if we make a habit of thinking for a few minutes every day, when small ideas come to us at different times and places, we should record them without neglecting them. Perhaps because these ideas are small, they may not make sense to us at the moment, but if we record these ideas regularly, we can find a chance to put the ideas together when we decide to take a longer time to think. It may be that these ideas do not fit together because they do not make sense to us. If we sit down and think and try to put everything together, we can come up with a big idea that can surprise us because the birthplace of big ideas is a collection of small ideas.

It is critical to also think about what we desire for ten or fifteen minutes before going to bed. In Micah 2:1,[133] it says, "Woe (judgment is coming) to those who devise wickedness and plot evil on their beds! When morning comes, they practice evil Because it is in the power of their hands." These men were not empowered to do evil by the thoughts of their day, but it was an idea that they thought and pondered before they lay down on their bed. Our conscious mind is a gatekeeper. It works only during daytime. But the main working time for our subconscious mind to organize thought and turn it into energy is when we are sleeping.

Our last-minute thoughts before bed are like giving our subconscious mind homework. Because our subconscious mind works on what is very important and what we want, it works all night, and when we wake up in the morning, it multiplies that thought and presents it to us. This is why many people go to sleep thinking they are tired and wake up tired in the morning. Even if we sleep for eight hours, if we spend the night thinking about fatigue, our mind keeps our body tired.

---

133 AMP

I always think about the things I want in life before I go to sleep. If I go to bed happily thinking about praying and reading the Word in the morning, my morning prayer is powerful. Many people find it difficult to pray in the morning because when they go to bed at night, they do not think of praying in the morning. If we go to bed thinking about what we want to happen during our prayer time, what often happens during our prayer time is the kind of idea we thought of at night.

Every Sunday before I preach, I talk to God's Spirit on Saturday night, and I dream about how I will preach the message I received from the Lord and how the Lord will use this weak person to do a great work. I sleep with great excitement. When I wake up in the morning, I see my spirit awakened and filled with the power to serve.

When I drive to church with my wife on Sunday mornings for early morning prayer, I am very careful to keep that message and enthusiasm inside me from disappearing. We often go on Sunday mornings without talking for a long minute. This is what I do to protect the spiritual thoughts that I have meditated on at night.

The Thought Respects Those Who Respect It

David's words always amaze me when I think about the power of ideas when he says, "How precious also are Your thoughts to me, O God! How great is the sum of them!" (Psalm 139:17).[134] I don't know any great man who does not respect the thought. When we look at any great man, one of the secrets of his greatness is his respect for ideas. The biggest sign of people who do not respect ideas is that they despise and disrespect other people's ideas. He who does not respect others' ideas does not respect himself.

Many times, when I listen to people's speeches, I am careful because their speech reflects their thoughts. When I see them belittling God's thoughts, I stay away from these people because not only do I know that that person can't get anywhere, but I also know that if he despises God's glorious purpose, he can trample on mine. There is no one who despises my thoughts and respects me. One expression of our respect for people is that we respect their opinions.

---

134 NKJV

I think one of the problems of our society is not respecting ideas. This is what we see in a meeting and forum. Even if it is right or wrong, an opinion should be respected. Life is a school where one can learn from correct ideas, and it is possible to learn by listening to wrong ideas and knowing what is wrong since we know from knowledge. Thinking that you know everything and speaking disparagingly of others is ignorance. When I think about the problem of people who do not have the practice of thinking noble thoughts, I wonder if it is the lack of habit of respecting thoughts as David said.

Mankind's greatest lifetime work is to connect one idea with another and seek a great idea to bring both earthly and spiritual life to a better level. If we don't try to understand the bigger idea by combining the ideas of the people of the same age and the ideas between generations, the ideas of one age and one generation alone can never change the world. The scientific advances we see today are because of the people who laid the foundation for the original ideas years ago. It is an inescapable fact that one idea is added to the other and makes a great contribution to where we are today.

When I listen to the conversations on Facebook and the media, even though I don't know the people, I feel sorry, wondering what kind of life they have in their inner world. The balance of life is not in speech but in thought. If the thought is quality and noble, that is what makes human speech acceptable and effective. Life is the product of many people's thoughts and can never be the result of just one person.

By choosing the right ones and learning from the wrong ones, we can speed up our progress and make life easier. But if there is a person who says that "only what I have said is right," it is doubtful that he even benefits himself, let alone society. Perhaps this person has an advanced degree in a subject, and while this may bring him a good salary, I never believe that he will have the ability to bring any change to society or the church. God is a God who respects ideas and shares His ideas. However, He shares His ideas only with those who respect His ideas. It is not possible to respect God while despising His thought.

Human Thought and God's Spirit

In Romans 9:1–2,[135] the apostle Paul said, "I am telling the truth in Christ, I am not lying, my conscience testifies with me [enlightened and prompted] by the Holy Spirit" to prove how great the burden of the people of Israel was and that even he himself was cursed apart from Christ. Another translation (NIV) says that "my conscience confirms it through the Holy Spirit." The Holy Spirit works with our conscience. The apostle Paul says that his noble thoughts and burdens of the people are correct. Not only he himself knows, but he also has the testimony of the Holy Spirit about this truth.

The Holy Spirit testifies not only to our conscience but also to our spirit. Romans 8:16[136] says, "The Spirit Himself testifies and confirms, together with our spirit [assuring us] that we [believers] are children of God." The easiest way to know whether we are right about what we think and whether our motives are right is to hear and know the testimony of the Spirit about that matter.

Another great work of the Spirit of God in the believer is to intercede with unspeakable groanings. But when He intercedes for us, He wants to see and know what is in our hearts. The greatest folly of man is to have an empty heart. That person who has no thoughts is lazy. God sees a person's heart or a person's thoughts before He starts doing anything in a person's life. Romans 8:26–27[137] states:

> In the same way the Spirit [comes to us and] helps us in our weakness. We do not know what prayer to offer or how to offer it as we should, but the Spirit Himself [knows our need and at the right time] intercedes on our behalf with sighs and groanings too deep for words. And He who searches the hearts knows what the mind of the Spirit is, because the Spirit intercedes [before God] on behalf of God's people in accordance with God's will.

When he says he examines the heart, this thought is the thought in our subconscious mind. When he gets that thought, the Holy Spirit relates his thought to God's thought and prays with groaning. No thought in

135 AMP
136 AMP
137 AMP

our heart means no tool for the Holy Spirit to work miracles. There is one question that stands out among the questions that Lord Jesus asked before He healed all people, "What do you want Me to do for you? Or do you want to be healed?" It was at the heart of these questions that the Lord was asking to know what was in their hearts. He cannot do or give what he does not have in his heart.

When we study the section up to 2 Chronicles 1:7–11, after Solomon's reign when God said to Solomon, "What shall I give you?" we see that Solomon asked for wisdom and knowledge. God immediately blessed Solomon not only with what he had asked for but with many other blessings. But in verse 11, we find the answer to Solomon's prayer and what caught God's attention; it is the word that says, "This was in your heart." What made God's heart happy and gave Solomon such a wonderful answer was not because Solomon was different but because he saw what he had been thinking in his heart for a long time. I think he must have thought that if he could get to the kingdom, he would ask God for wisdom.

When he sees what is in man's mind, the Lord rises to do anything for man. This human thought can be reduced, expanded, or narrowed. He opened His heart to Solomon like the sand of the sea (thoughts were given to Him like the sand of the sea). Our minds have a natural tendency to expand and contract; this means that he can handle or understand many things at once. He may have the ability to see things far ahead and think broadly and deeply. A broad-minded person has the capacity and ability to see things not only from one perspective but from different perspectives.

As a Christian, reading the Word of God and reading other spiritual books will broaden our horizons. When we read books, we don't just read the text. What we see and share is the writer's thoughts. How he looks at a topic differently from what we see and the flow of his thoughts, analysis, conclusion, and life-long experiences, we can share that knowledge just by reading it in a short time.

God wrote the Bible to share His thoughts with us. Many people read but do not understand the Bible; this is because they only read the letters. The Bible is written in the form of letters, but it is the thought of God. This is why Jesus said to the Pharisees and Sadducees, who were strong in the knowledge of the Scriptures, "You are mistaken, not knowing the Scriptures nor the power of God" (Matthew 22:29).[138] The main problem with saying you don't know the Scriptures you read is that you don't understand the thought of God and why the Scriptures are written.

Our mind builds itself with thoughts. Deliberate thinking helps to get a flow of thought. Respecting other people's ideas and sharing other people's ideas expands the horizon of our thought. Above all, it is wisdom and the existence to respect and accept God's thought that is subtle and big in His thoughts.

138 NKJV

Chapter 11—Meditation and Deep Thought

Joshua 1:8[139]:

> This Book of the Law shall not depart from your mouth, but you shall read [and meditate on] it day and night, so that you may be careful to do [everything] in accordance with all that is written in it; for then you will make your way prosperous, and then you will be successful.

Proverbs 20:5 says, "Counsel in the heart of man is like deep water, but a man of understanding will draw it out." The Amplified Bible translation of this idea is that "a plan (motive, wise counsel) in the heart of a man is like water in a deep well, but a man of understanding draws it out." When he says that a person with understanding digs out, the American Standard Version says that he who "[counsels] in the heart of man is like a deep water." The New International Version is that "the purposes of a person's heart are deep waters, but one who has insight draws them out."

Thought is like an ocean. Its breadth, length, height, and depth are immeasurable. For one who has gone deep, he can draw from the deep. Those who can draw are those who give time to think and meditate. A person's ability to understand is like giving time to meditate. A person who does not have time to meditate is one who does not value understanding. As we have seen above, the type of thought depends on the length, breadth, height, and depth of our meditation on a subject with oneself. The quality and type of the result depend on the time we give to meditation and the maturity and type of meditation. If we can meditate, our ability to create and accomplish what we want is high.

Meditation has three stages. The first one is to think about what we want in our mind over and over again. The second is to say softly to

---

139 AMP

ourselves what we have meditated on. The third is where we say out loud what we have meditated on, just like a lion roars when it is satisfied. Once, D. L. Moody said, "When God taught Joshua how to be conqueror, he taught him how to handle the word, but not how to handle the sword." Joshua 1:8,[140] "This Book of the Law shall not depart from your mouth, but you shall read [and meditate on] it day and night, so that you may be careful to do [everything] in accordance with all that is written in it; for then you will make your way prosperous, and then you will be successful."

Meditation has its own principles. We will see the two principles of meditation clearly in this section. One is to think about it day and night, and the other is to confess the book of the law. The strong word on both ideas is that it will not depart from your mouth day and night. This meditation shows how much concentration and practice it takes to keep the flow of thought flowing. To think day and night requires constant thinking. It shows how much attention it takes to accompany what we meditate on with words. It is the book of the law that commands us to think. This means that meditation requires prior reading and knowledge. The primitive root word of meditation in Hebrew, *hagah*, means one is to roar, speak, utter, mutter, murmur (in pleasure or anger), study, imagine and ponder. The other meaning for meditation is "mental enthusiasm."

As a Christian, without the Word of God, meditation is weak. A mind that does not reflect is fruitless and barren. It cannot generate anything. What we believe and say determines how we live our lives. Solar radiation loses its energy because the radiation from the sun is scattered before it reaches us. If the sun's rays reached the earth without scattering, they would have the power to melt the entire world in a few minutes. When we were children, we used to burn dried leaves with a glass beam. The leaf is on the ground and does not burn when the sun's rays touch it. The difference is that the glass collects the sun's rays and sends them to the leaf, so the leaf has no choice but to burn.

Such is the power of meditation. We can see the power of meditation when we gather our thoughts and focus on one thing. Life is not about what we do but what we think and speak. The question is knowing the kind of meditation and speech that brings fulfillment.

---

140 AMP

Joshua's victory is to meditate on the book of the law both day and night, and the benefit of meditating on it is that it empowers him to keep the word of the law. When He says that no one will stand against him during his life, He warns him to think about it and not to separate the law from his mouth. Performance is not a matter of chance but of choice. It is not questionable that our choice is something that we have deliberately given time to think about and speak about. Meditation is an inner process. Speaking is the power of commanding what we contemplate to come and be seen in the real world. We confirm our thoughts with our words. Meditation is like pregnancy. Speaking is giving birth to what we have conceived. A man who meditates but does not speak is like a woman whose child is dead inside.

The thought we give birth to is the same kind we conceive. For this reason, the Bible tells us about the things we should think about in order to have a proper pregnancy of thoughts. The apostle Paul invites us to embrace the ideas that are there by saying, "Think about these things." What Philippians 4:8 says when he says, "Think these things" is to show that we can choose our thoughts, and by putting in what we want, we can put out what we do not want. Action is the consummation of thought, so the kind of thought we think determines the type and extent of our actions. As Christians, meditating not only on good thoughts but also on spiritual thoughts allows us to live a spiritual life by increasing our spiritual feelings and spiritual capacities. God's Word is tested; it tells us about the things we should think about in life. It is possible to live and experience a spiritual life by deliberately thinking about spiritual things. Spiritual secrets are revealed to those who meditate on the Word of God.

Spiritual life depends on thinking and meditating on spiritual things. Romans 8:5 says that minding the flesh brings death, but minding the Spirit tells us that we can find peace and life. We know that there are people in our world who do not have a lot of peace and happiness and will do a lot to find peace and happiness. But peace and happiness are found within, not without. Peace is the result of inner thoughts, not external material things. True peace is found by thinking about the Word of God or thinking about spiritual things. It is found by thinking of the Lord Jesus, who is the true peace and king of peace. That is why it is written in the Psalm that "I have thought of God, and I am glad."

Matthew 15:18[141] says, "But whatever [word] comes out of the mouth comes from the heart, and this is what defiles and dishonors the man." Evil thoughts, murder, fornication, adultery, theft, and slander in the name of false witness arise from the heart, and these are the ones that defile a person. Everything originates from the human heart. Its source is in the human heart or thought. It is not what a person says or does. It is in the source of his heart. If we change bad thoughts with good thoughts, our heart will be a source of good things.

Power is in thought and not in action; people need to have time to think if they want the energy to do it. Usually evil or good, blessing or curse, disease or health, wealth or poverty starts from what we meditate on. The source of all things is in the thought of man. Being able to meditate correctly is the source of the path and power to live the right life. A man should not labor for work but for thought. Change comes from the power of deep thought, not the result of effort and fatigue. Work is the product of thought. It is worth working for. But a work done without thought is labor. It is only then that a person who is able to meditate gains the ability to work hard.

Reflection and Thought Patterns

When we think of a thought over and over again, thought patterns are created in our mind. If these patterns are imprinted on our minds in the form of habits, our thoughts will have the ability to always follow that habitual pattern, even in times of happiness and sadness. If the pattern is negative, even if something good happens, we will be forced to feel sad, or if the pattern is positive, even if something bad happens, we will have the ability to rejoice. This is the difference between carnal and spiritual man and mind. A spiritual person sees things in any situation of life according to the pattern of thoughts that God's Word has already formed in his mind. The response to all things will be according to the pattern of his thoughts. The natural man's mind will react according to the pattern of his thoughts.

Meditation is a life force. This power works continuously twenty-four hours a day. We have seen that at least sixty thousand thought waves pass

---

141 AMP

through our mind in a single day. But we can identify only those thoughts and feelings that we deliberately think. How wonderful are God's riches? He has graciously given our mind this ability to process more than sixty thousand thoughts in a single day. Man's work is only to consider what is good and God's thoughts.

This is why human thought is said to be like deep water. To copy from this deep sixty thousand thoughts, it takes time to think and meditate and think only the good ones. God does not give us a picture of one truth at a time, but He constantly gives us a glimpse of the image. It is the reward of the meditator to connect these wild ideas and find their meaning. Contemplatives say that it is revealed to us as soon as we see the picture assembled. What is revealed is not the bringing of an idea that we did not have but the end of the connected idea. The joy of this revelation is beyond words.

In Isaiah 28:9–10[142] it says, "Whom will he teach knowledge? and whom will he make to understand the message? them that are weaned from the milk, and drawn from the breasts? For it is precept upon precept, precept upon precept; line upon line, line upon line; here a little, there a little."

In this part, God wanted to teach the people, just like a weaned baby. He wanted to teach them by giving a few commands here and there, but they despised this and returned to the prophet, who told them they had fallen and were doomed to death. Yes, this is how God works. Little here, little there, line upon line, precept upon precept. He does not spread out all the ideas at once. Even if He did, we wouldn't be able to understand it. Every now and then, He gives us a few ideas and sees that we are faithful to that idea and spend time pondering it. After that, He adds another to the idea He gave us and brings us to the full and complete idea. This is the main way God has given to mankind.

It is not a requirement to be rich or intelligent to think. He does not charge anyone to go to school or pay anything. Any sane person can meditate. If everyone who thinks can concentrate his thoughts, that thought will inevitably turn into action as a force. Wealth, knowledge, character change, spirituality, and success all start with choosing and focusing on

---

142 ASV

ideas. This is what creates a thought pattern in our mind and creates a fence to prevent us from living life outside of it. Satan keeps people's minds from thinking many things because he knows that if they start meditating, it will be easy, and they will be successful.

Meditation and the Parable of the Sower

The main message of the parable of the sower in Matthew 13:18–23[143] is about meditation. The seed that fell by the wayside was uprooted because he did not pay any attention to the message he heard of God. As soon as the Word of God is sown in their minds, the evil one snatches it away because he knows the power of meditation. "The seed falling on rocky ground refers to someone who hears the word and at once receives it with joy. But since they have no root, they last only a short time. When trouble or persecution comes because of the word, they quickly fall away." This shows us that when we meditate, we should stay and meditate until the Word takes root in us. A person who does not understand and does this will stumble in times of trouble.

"The seed falling among the thorns refers to someone who hears the word, but the worries of this life and the deceitfulness of wealth choke the word making it unfruitful" (Matthew 13:22).[144] The problem with this third person is that they want to live with two unrelated ideas at the same time: the Word of God and the desire of this world's wealth. As the verse shows us, it shows how the desire of wealth can choke the seeded Word of God and make it not bear fruit. "The seed falling on good soil refers to someone who hears the word and understands it. This is the one who produces a crop, yielding thirty, sixty and a hundred times what was sown" (Matthew 13:23).[145]

It is the place where the seed is planted that makes the seed grow. The soil allows the seed to enter, provides moisture, and gives it a chance to bear fruit. There is no problem with the seed but with the heart in which it sows. The good land yielded thirty, sixty, and a hundredfold. What makes the land good is that it creates a suitable environment for

---

143 NIV
144 NIV
145 NIV

the seed. The way to take care of any idea, natural or spiritual, is to give it time and nurture it by meditation until it takes root and bears fruit.

The problem of all three is that they do not listen and meditate to the words of the kingdom. Here, the words "lack of understanding" relate to "he plucks up what is sown in the heart." He says that he will snatch away the word that was sown; the enemy snatches away his thoughts before he reaches his mind and spirit or ignores it. The great benefit of meditation is not just to help us understand ideas; it has a deeper meaning than that. When any idea enters our spirit, it first passes through our mind. Since the will of man is in the soul, we will never be able to bring down the thoughts that we have not decided to accept into our spirit and gain spiritual understanding. One of the great benefits of meditation is that it gives us the ability to bring thought down from our mind to our spirit. The mind is the main entrance to spiritual things.

Proverbs 19:21[146] says, "There are many plans in a man's heart, Nevertheless the LORD's counsel that will stand." This passage shows that the human heart is blessed with many thoughts. It is stated that he should not only think about the thoughts in his heart but also think about what is stable and what is not stable among these thoughts. All the people who lived with unsustainable thoughts made their lives on earth useless. They passed by without any influential lives. Among many ideas, knowing what God's is and thinking about it, all those who have lived have done great deeds and passed away as great men.

Human greatness is based on choosing and deliberately thinking about big ideas. Once a person is able to think again and again about a chosen idea, God will turn that chosen idea into reality. In the same way, if that person's chosen idea is evil, Satan will use that evil idea for evil.

God's goodness is expressed by giving many and great thoughts to man. The greatness of a person depends on the thoughts he receives and deals with. The thought invitations are many, so it is up to us to choose what we want. A person who enters a restaurant to eat is not served a meal first but is given a list of the types of food he wants to eat. The first job of the waiters is to present the person with a list of food items. If that person does not state his food preferences in any way, he cannot be served

---

146 NKJV

food. Although the restaurant can offer many types of food, no food can be served until the diner chooses the type of food he wants. Likewise, God presents more than sixty thousand thoughts to our minds every day. Although he has the ability to propose and do all kinds of ideas, he cannot do anything unless we choose. Every thought that goes through our minds is not only of God. This is why when we meditate, we must first choose what to meditate on.

Such is life then. Thinking an idea, choosing an idea, and living by thinking about the idea we have chosen and making a pattern in our mind are given to everyone without discrimination so that we can live the life we want to live. This is why we cannot give any reason when we come before the Lord. All our lives start from our inner thoughts, and there is no one on earth who has not been blessed by God. Deliberately developing the habit of thinking and meditating every day makes us like a person who lifts the weight of life from the head. In both our physical and spiritual lives, devoting time to purposeful meditation is a life principle that makes the small man great and the fruitless man fruitful. Our world of life depends on the thought we receive for meditation.

Chapter 12—Thoughts and Words, Words and Action

Luke 24:19,[147] "And He said to them, 'What things?' So they said to Him, 'The things concerning Jesus of Nazareth, who was a Prophet mighty in deed and word before God and all the people.'"

Words and actions are equal in scale. They should also have the same position. Words are worthless if they are not backed up by actions. Action has no meaning if it is not accompanied by words. Both together spark with beauty. But when there is only one, the balance is skewed. Beauty steals, and it loses meaning. As Jude wrote in his epistle, it will be like clouds without water; if a cloud appears, it is necessary and appropriate to pour water. If not, it is just an idea that is not expressed verbally or a word that is not expressed in action.

In the life and ministry of the Lord Jesus, if there is one thing that is said to be a great memorial, it is that His words and actions are the same. Not only the same, but Luke said He was powerful in both. When soldiers were sent to Jesus and returned, their testimony about Jesus was amazing. They said that they had never heard anyone speak like this. His speeches were powerful and full of authority. One of the things that gave power to His speech was that He expressed His speech in action. The ministry of the Lord Jesus was strong and powerful both in words and deeds before man and God. This was one of the secrets of the service's success.

Thought and Word

A word is a combination of verbal sounds, which is a manifestation of an idea and is spoken by the human ear. Any word is based on an idea. When we speak words, the main purpose is to express the thoughts in our mind. Without thoughts, there are no words. We can identify a person's

147 NKJV

identity by listening to his speech. Because a person thinks, if he speaks his thoughts, then the word is a manifestation of a person's inner thoughts or a manifestation of a person's inner world. Words and thoughts are two sides of the same coin. If there is no thought, we cannot utter a word.

James 3:2 says that spiritual maturity is measured by our speech. In particular, the Amplified Bible translation says:

> For we all stumble and sin in many ways. If anyone does not stumble in what he says [never saying the wrong thing], he is a perfect man [fully developed in character, without serious flaws], able to bridle his whole body and rein in his entire nature [taming his human faults and weaknesses].

A spiritually mature person is known for his speech. The manifestation of the inner self is the word. A man's life is governed by the little oar of his tongue. James describes the function of the word in two verbs. One is "to control," and the other is "to lead." James 3:3–4[148] says:

> Now if we put bits into the horses' mouths to make them obey us, we guide their whole body as well. And look at the ships. Even though they are so large and are driven by strong winds, they are still directed by a very small rudder wherever the impulse of the helmsman determines.

The reasons we put the bridle in the mouth of horses are it is one way to make them obey, and the other is to lead them where we want. We lead them with a little bridle, controlling their body. Ships, no matter how large, are driven by strong winds and go where the will of the captain takes them. The ship's license is held not by its size but by its leader.

With a small oar, the great ship is steered. The oars that the captain can turn to steer the rudder in the direction he wants are very small compared to the size of the ship. However, a thing as large as a ship is only a small oar that keeps a force as great as a storm from going astray.

The word of Jacob tells us the same. Although this verse is talking about teachers, it shows us that the words we speak are important to lead our lives in the direction we want. Self-control is associated with speech. A horse's power can be tamed with a bridle. That is a verbal example. Expressing or declaring what we think is the main part of life. Life is

148 AMP

governed and guided by words. We can control and lead life, and the way to roll the big rock of life is to speak words. Words are the reflection of thoughts, and if our speech agrees with our thoughts, there can never be any power that escapes from the two.

We have seen in James 3:2 that maturity in the spiritual world is measured by our words. Some translations say that he is a mature person who does not stumble with words. Most of our mistakes in life are related to our thoughts and our tongues. The problem with a lack of self-control is the problem of not controlling one's thoughts and speech. Losing the direction of life and not being able to go where we want is a problem of thinking and words.

The maturity of a spiritual person does not depend on saying whatever he wants. Some people who teach the greatness of the power of words appear to be extreme. This means that if we say everything we want repeatedly, we will get it. Not only is this false, but it is also unspiritual and unbiblical. In Hebrews 13:5–6[149] we see, "He has said, 'I WILL NEVER [under any circumstances] DESERT YOU [nor give you up nor leave you without support, nor will I in any degree leave you helpless], NOR WILL I FORSAKE or LET YOU DOWN or RELAX MY HOLD ON YOU [assuredly not]!'" The true meaning of confession of the Bible is clearly stated in this verse. The basis of what we say is not what we want but what God says. Because He said…we say. The power of our words lies in what God says. The ability to boldly say, "I'm not afraid; what people will do to me is based on God's promise saying, 'I will never forsake or leave you.' Spiritual results are achieved by speaking the same word by faith that God has already said."

The thoughts of our hearts and the words of our mouths should be in harmony to guide our lives in the direction we want. No matter how great the pressure of the wind is, the direction of the ship is determined by a small oar. The secret of living life is to shape our thoughts with God's words and say those words repeatedly so that we don't drift in the direction of life's waves. A mature person's speech is seasoned with grace. Their words are edifying, not destructive. As a person matures, he is careful about what he thinks and speaks. But when he is not careful,

---

149 AMP

his thoughts and speech will be pessimistic and fruitless. You only have to listen to people to know what they are thinking. Our speech reveals us.

One thing Satan wanted from Job was his tongue. When he was brought before God, if you took what he had, he would insult you. The Bible testifies about Job and says, "But Job did not sin with his lips."[150] Job prevented Satan from getting what he wanted. His plan was to deceive Job by using his mouth. The enemy's attempt to twist the course of his life failed, so he went to his wife. And the wife said, "Have you kept your integrity yet?" She told him to curse God and die. One of the reasons Job was not cursed by God was because his thinking about God was right. Job's integrity protected him from insults. This is what we call the harmony of thoughts of our hearts and the words of our mouths.

Why is the insult necessary? The mark of a mature person is his word, and his word is the bridle and leader of his life. Job saw his wife as one of the foolish women and was defeated by her words. He met the woman who had lived with him all those years and bore him all those children; he did not know her until the speech that was revealed in the storm of life. It is speech that reveals people. What reveals their thinking is their speech. And their thinking is known when they are shaken by the waves of life.

Our problems in life reveal who each person is, whether he has put anything into his mind. It is at such times that who we are is revealed not only to others but to ourselves. Although God is omniscient, He allows various problems to pass through our lives to reveal what is in our hearts. Deuteronomy 8:2[151] says, "And you shall remember [always] all the ways which the LORD your God has led you these forty years in the wilderness, so that He might humble you and test you, to know what was in your heart (mind), whether you would keep His commandments or not."

Verbal and Mental Agreement

This world we live in was created and sustained by words, and it is only by these words that we are held together to each other. As the writer of Hebrews tells us, it is not only connected to each other but supported by the word. God not only created and supported this world but also

---

150 Job 1:22
151 AMP

established the system of this world through words. Science itself supports that there is no question that our world is full of words.

Scientists say that words are the electromagnetic and quantum life energy that we create with our thoughts. These are what we have decided and created while thinking in our minds over time. When we say negative words, we spray negative chemicals. And when we say the positive, we spray positive chemicals. These chemicals control our thoughts and grow stronger in our brains.

If we constantly think and talk about them, our mind will inevitably make our attitude and future outlook negative, and it will even go so far as to oppose God's thoughts and truth by creating a strong fortress in our mind. By repeatedly thinking and speaking positive thoughts, we gain the ability to change our behavior and all our bad habits. Our life is the result of two things: one is our thoughts, and the other is our speech. When our thoughts are beautiful, our words become beautiful. When our words are beautiful, our life will be beautiful.

A word has the power to determine a person's destiny until it ignites the race of creation. Second Timothy 2:14[152] states, "Remind the people of these facts, and solemnly charge them in the presence of God to avoid petty controversy over words, which does no good, and [upsets and undermines and] ruins [the faith of] those who listen." In the same chapter, verse 17 states that the teaching or word that comes out of a person's mouth will eat as doth a gangrene. It speaks of the great power of words as cancer eats away at the human body.

The source of everything visible is the invisible. The words we speak are revealed; the thoughts we think and what we believe are internal. When the two agree, life responds appropriately. The fruit of a tree is the visible part. The secret of the fruit lies in its invisible root. That is why the Lord said to change the tree so that the fruit would be good. The Lord said this about the change of human identity. If we associate our identity with an idea, the basis for seeing the right fruit by looking at the example is to be under the right tree. In other words, if a person's words are the result of thoughts, to beautify the words, beautifying the thoughts should be the primary task.

---

152 AMP

PART FIVE

Chapter 13—Thinking and Spirituality

Hebrews 13:18,[153] "Keep praying for us, for we are convinced that we have a good conscience, seeking to conduct ourselves honorably [that is, with moral courage and personal integrity] in all things."

What is spirituality? What makes Christianity different from others? There are many religions in the world. All of them show man's efforts to reach God, but Christianity is very special because it shows what God has done for man by sending His only Son. All religions are based on human effort, but Christianity is based on what Christ did. Religion teaches people what to do, but Christianity teaches what Christ did. All religions are based on the actions of the believers, but Christianity focuses on the actions of the Savior.

For New Testament believers, the life that God has given us in Christ is amazing and difficult to imagine with the human mind. The Lord who gave us the Christian life instructed us in His Word to live a great life of salvation. I do not doubt that in every believer there is a zeal to live for God and honor Him, but the problem is living the truth of what you know. If Christ Jesus has finished His work, then salvation is complete. If only faith is needed to be saved, not work, then what made it difficult to live?

In my opinion, the problem of many believers is the same. Whether it's from the religion we come from or the upbringing we grew up in, we all believe and know that grace has saved us through faith. What we don't seem to know is the way to live the life given to us by Christ and to change our thinking or renew our mind. The foundation of true discipleship is the same. It is a change of thinking. We accept that we

---

153 AMP

believe in the salvation of the Spirit. We do not have to do anything but believe to be saved. But to live that life given to us by Christ, there is a great work that should be recognized by every believer. This work is to raise and develop the mindset and attitude to live the new life. Christianity consists of three things: salvation of the Spirit, change of mind, and Christ-like living.

An identity crisis is a problem of not understanding the truth. If a person lives like an animal while being recognized as a human being, the problem is an identity problem. It is easier to live Christianity when we know what Christ has done for us and who we are. When I say that it is easy to live Christianity, I do not mean that Christianity is lived by human ability. It is to show that we should know what is the work and responsibility of man. Christianity is a life lived by the power of the Holy Spirit and a changed mind. The Holy Spirit's power is manifested in the believer according to the believer's knowledge of the Word of God and the believer's willingness of heart.

The Word is the sword of the Spirit. The Holy Spirit expresses His power according to His Word. It is difficult for the Holy Spirit to work in a person who does not have the Word and who has not changed his mind by the truth of the Word. In order to live a true Christian life, the greatest task of a Christian's life is to renew and change his mind according to the Word of God. The more our minds are changed according to the Word of God, the greater our ability to imitate the Lord. A transformed mind is the life of a disciple.

In Romans 12:1–2[154] it says:

> I beseech you therefore, brethren, by the mercies of God, that you present your bodies a living sacrifice, holy, acceptable to God, which is your reasonable service. And do not be conformed to this world, but be transformed by the renewing of your mind, that you may prove what is that good and acceptable and perfect will of God.

The apostle Paul emphatically exhorts all believers to first be transformed by the renewing of their minds. He says that being like the world is a matter of thinking, not a matter of living, so be transformed by the

154 NKJV

renewal of your mind. Change begins with thought. What we change is the way we think. This is why it says to test and know the good, acceptable, and perfect will of God. Before a Christian begins to live Christianity, he must shape his thinking according to the truth of God's Word and change his thinking pattern. Our life is like our thought pattern.

In Romans 6:17–18[155] it says:

> But thank God that though you were slaves of sin, you became obedient with all your heart to the standard of teaching in which you were instructed and to which you were committed. And having been set free from sin, you have become the slaves of righteousness [of conformity to God's will and purpose].

In other translations it means God be praised that you obey the teaching given to you with all your heart even though you were slaves to sin. It also translates that you have been freed from sin and become slaves to righteousness. It is clearly seen that the apostle is not announcing their freedom from the slavery of sin through work struggle; instead, he asserts that the great power of their liberation was a form of education for those who gave themselves. This lesson certainly changed their thinking.

That is why he brought them out of the slavery of sin to become slaves of righteousness. It is this teaching that we call a higher thought. In both directions, living a righteous life and living a sinful life is the basis of the teaching that we have been given to ourselves. Knowledge shapes thinking. It changes our lives on the way we see things or the knowledge we get through education. After being saved in Christianity, one of the most important lessons is to see that God sees us and declares freedom by considering ourselves to be who we are. This changes our actions, and it is the destiny of those who have learned the higher knowledge of God's will.

The kind of education we are given is the kind of life we live. Knowing the Word is not enough. It requires changing the pattern of our thoughts according to the Word. A person who changes his thoughts according to the Word of God will not have a problem of living according to that same Word. The greatest work of the Christian life is to form a spiritual mind

---

155 AMP

and not to struggle to live a spiritual life. When my thoughts and my life are the same, it clearly shows what I have learned and what I believe.

One of the key words in the book of Romans is "consider." When the apostle talks about the Christian life, he uses the words "we know and believe." In Romans 6:8–9, and in verse 11, he uses the word: "'Consider/reckon' that you are dead to sin but alive to God in Christ Jesus, our Lord." The meaning of the word "consider" usually is "to accept something as certain and as the source of information that we use to prove something."

On the other hand, it also refers to thinking about what we want to be before we become who we are. As we can understand from these meanings, we can get four major lessons: knowing and understanding with certainty that we are alive in the Lord Jesus, that the information given to us is correct, mental preparation or mind renewal, and acting or practicing.

The most important piece of knowledge is that the Lord Jesus is alive. Our faith should be founded on who the Lord Jesus is and not on what we do. First and foremost, our lives are not proof that we are alive. The foundation of our Christian life should be on believing that Jesus is alive and made us alive. A person who accepts this reality in his mind and meditates on it repeatedly has embraced that higher thought, and his path will follow his notion.

Christianity is not about straggling; it is about reckoning. He who wants to live must learn to reckon. Living becomes easier when we start considering. To live without reckoning is to be bitter. The point is not what I do but what is done to me. When I know and reflect on what has been done to me, I create a mental pattern. Once I form a thought pattern, the hardest part is living off that thought and not doing it.

In Romans 4:5[156] it is written, "But to him who does not work but believes on Him who justifies the ungodly, his faith is accounted for righteousness." As we have seen above, the word "consider" shows an act of faith in a truth. This means that what God said about me is bigger than my action. My faith determines my path, but my life does not prove my faith. The reason why I say that is because it is possible not to believe while living. It is impossible not to live when we believe.

---

156 NKJV

When my mind aligns with God's truth, my action also aligns with God's truth. My mistakes in living the truth with a changed mind will please God more than the right life I live with an unconverted mind. In order for action to be the result of faith, the mind must know the truth, accept it, and meditate on it.

Thought, Action, and Noble Life

Hebrews 13:18[157] says, "Keep praying for us, for we are convinced that we have a good conscience, seeking to conduct ourselves honorably [that is, with moral courage and personal integrity] in all things." Some interpretations say that we follow this in order to have a good conscience to live a life that is honorable in everything, while others say that we know that we have a good conscience in order to live a righteous life in all things. Regardless of the interpretation, the main message is that the way to live a good or honorable life is to have a good conscience.

The success of Paul's and his partner's life did not just happen. The secret of their lives was their commitment to creating the right consciousness or thinking in which they found an identity that does the right thing. When they dedicated themselves to living a life that is honorable in everything, they changed their conscience or their thinking. Beyond their own efforts, we see them looking for a prayer partner to pray for them.

This shows us how much they strived to create the right mindset or conscience to live a dignified life. If we look at the verse carefully, it says that we will follow this to have a good conscience to live a dignified life (to live a higher life) or to live the life that God has given us in Christ. This word we follow shows us that it is something they are interested in and paying attention to. They changed the world with their lives and service because their focus was on creating the right and honorable mind or way of thinking.

It is enough to look at the third chapter of Philippians to see how these early saints thought highly about living a higher life. In this chapter, the apostle Paul expressed the height of his thinking by writing, "I want to know Christ—yes, to know the power of his resurrection and participation in his sufferings, becoming like him in his death" (Philip-

---

157 AMPC

pians 3:10).[158] Look what he is saying. He set the height of the glory of life that he wanted to live by accepting suffering like Christ Jesus, dying, and then rising like Jesus.

In verse 12[159] he said, "Not that I have already obtained all this, or have already arrived at my goal, but I press on to take hold of that for which Christ Jesus took hold of me." And in verse 15,[160] "Let us therefore, as many as be perfect, be thus minded: and if in anything ye be otherwise minded, God shall reveal even this unto you." The Amplified Bible translation said that "all of us who are mature [pursuing spiritual perfection] should have this attitude, and if in any respect you have a different attitude, God will make that clear to you."

The difference between the mature Christian and the immature Christian is their mindset. The great advice that the apostle Paul gave to people who want to grow to spiritual maturity is about the mindset or attitude they should have. The word "attitude" means "a settled way of thinking." Our mindset or settled way of thinking is the main reason to lay hold of the glorious life that God has prepared for us in Christ Jesus. The path of perfect people and people who are eager to reach perfection is to change their minds and be renewed by the spirit of their minds.

It is written in Ephesians 4:17–18[161]:

So this I say, and solemnly affirm together with the Lord [as in His presence], that you must no longer live as the [unbelieving] Gentiles live, in the futility of their minds [and in the foolishness and emptiness of their souls], for their [moral] understanding is darkened and their reasoning is clouded; [they are] alienated and self-banished from the life of God [with no share in it; this is] because of the [willful] ignorance and spiritual blindness that is [deep-seated] within them, because of the hardness and insensitivity of their heart.

---

158 NIV
159 NIV
160 KJV
161 AMP

And in verses 22–23,[162] he says:

> That, regarding your previous way of life, you put off your old self [completely discard your former nature], which is being corrupted through deceitful desires, and be continually renewed in the spirit of your mind [having a fresh, untarnished mental and spiritual attitude].

The reason why the Gentiles are far from the life of God is because they walk in the vanity of their minds. This mental futility is caused by not accepting the truth of the gospel. Other translations have said that "you were taught to live your old self,"[163] and in verse 23, "you are transformed by the renewing of your mind." It translates as "put on (be) the new man created in the likeness of God."

In this part, the apostle says that we were taught to live our Adamic natural selves. This means that when a baby is born, they learn how to live life in their body. They learn from their parents and the environment. It is the influence of the family and environment that makes them live the way they live. A parent teaches a girl to live like a girl and a boy like a boy, but when they are still children, they don't even know the difference between a boy and a girl. Living as a man and a woman is the result of shaping the family mentality. If there was a child living in a society where men wore skirts, he would live like that because his life would be according to his thoughts. A woman wears a dress because society's mentality has shaped the children's attitude.

In the same way, we used to accept that this is what we learned from our physical parents and society, and this is the worldly and carnal way of life and thinking. But now, being renewed in the spirit of our mind, live the kind of life that the new man who is given the righteousness of God should live. He says to put off the old thinking and put on the new thinking. It is possible to live the inner potential of the new person's life by knowing the identity of the new person from the Word, and it is necessary to follow and change our thinking to live a life that is honorable in everything like Paul.

---

162 AMP
163 NCV

All those who believe in Christ and are saved have spiritual life. To live that spiritual life, we must change our thinking. This, in Paul's words, explains that when we change our minds, we put off our old flesh and put on our new self, which is like Christ. Therefore, a Christian can live like Christ only if he is learning the teachings of Christ. He says, "You did not learn Christ that way in order to live in the new identity." The writer of Hebrews, in chapter 13 verse 18, says that we understand that we have a good conscience in order to live well in all things.

Christianity is the transition from one identity (old) to another (new), where we take off the old like a garment and put on the new and live in the image of Christ. This is a change of thinking referred to as the renewal of the heart. The simple thing in life is to live who you are. When we accept Christ, the identity of the new person is within, and his identity is Christ-like and has the capacity to live in Christianity. The Christian life is not one in which we strive to be what we are not but a life in which we realize who we are and experience who we are. That is why the apostle Paul said to train yourself unto godliness.

Life is not about struggling to live but practicing who we are. If we struggle, it shows that our thinking is still trying to be. This makes life difficult because it is impossible to be what we are not. Accustoming ourselves to live what we have is a different mindset. It begins with being, and the act is practice, not struggle.

In many of our churches today, the spiritual life that God gave us in Christ is not seen in the believer. This is because believers are not properly taught that they have this great spiritual life. If believers were given this knowledge to shape their way of thinking and live their identity, the old man would not have been empowered, and the new man would not have been afflicted. True Christian teaching is not a race for identity. If we knew that we are the children of God when we believe in Christ, that we are spiritual by accepting the righteousness of Christ, and if we were given the knowledge to exercise and live that identity, our churches would be filled with true and Christ-like disciples.

It is very important to teach that the spiritual life that God gave us in Christ is in the believer. It is important for believers to know that they do not have to struggle to live but to exercise the life of Christ that they have received from God by faith. If they began to practice living by the help of the Holy Spirit in the life they were given, the old man would die, and the new man would be renewed.

Thought and Holiness

Christianity is the free life we have found in Christ. We have seen that the change in life is not about finding identity but practicing identity. From the point of view of Romans chapters 6 and 12, our intention is to use it and not let it use us. The habit of deliberate thinking and meditation and the ability to direct our thoughts to what we want gives us the ability to control and calm when the desires of sin come like a storm.

In 1 Peter 4:1–2[164] it says, "Therefore, since Christ suffered for us in the flesh, arm yourselves also with the same mind, for he who has suffered in the flesh has ceased from sin, that he no longer should live the rest of his time in the flesh for the lusts of men, but for the will of God." The Amplified Bible translation says to arm yourselves with this thought as a warrior. He uses thought as a military weapon. An armed man is not easily defeated. The enemy's greatest plan is to disarm first. If he does that, it is easy to defeat the warrior. If the enemy takes away the armor of our thoughts, committing sin is inevitable.

Look what Peter said in verse 2, "arm yourselves also with the same mind." This is the mind that Christ had when He suffered in the flesh. The reason Christ Jesus has ceased sinning is the mindset He had. The enemy fights us with the thought of sin. We also fight back against that thought with the righteous thought or the mind that we have already renewed. Thought is the greatest weapon in the spiritual world.

First Peter 2:11[165] says, "Beloved, I beg you as sojourners and pilgrims, abstain from fleshly lusts which war against the soul." According to the Amplified Bible translation, "I urge you as aliens and strangers [in this world] to abstain from the sensual urges [those dishonorable desires] that wage war against the soul." When the enemy launches a campaign of war with evil intentions, the believer's response to war is according to the righteous thoughts he already holds. Sin reigns over man when

164 NKJV
165 NKJV

we are overcome by our souls. When the soul loses the battle, the flesh expresses it through action. The type of action reveals the type of thought we are defeated by. This is why God told Cain that "its desire is for you [to overpower you], but you must master it" (Genesis 4:7).[166] To rule and dominate is for the one who can overcome his thoughts first. If there is a desire to overcome, there is an expectation of Cain's action.

The power of sin is broken from our lives. Only when we have the thought to fight against it can we exercise the victory. One of the things that the Lord Jesus did to overcome death on the cross was the preparation of his mind to accept the suffering in His body. First Peter 2:22–23[167] says, "Who committed no sin, nor was deceit found in His mouth; who, when He was reviled, did not revile in return; when He suffered, He did not threaten, but committed Himself to Him who judges righteously." He showed us that He honored His Father by doing God's will because His response to every sinful invitation that was offered to Him was according to His thoughts. The Word touches my heart because when a person with inner strength is treated badly, he is insulted and suffers, and the response is not by doing the same or more. Rather, his response is to destroy the enemy's weapons with his preconceived idea of righteousness and surrender himself victoriously to the One who will judge him righteously. This is what it means to live a life of high holiness and honor for the one who can overcome in this way.

First Peter 2:21[168] says, "For [as a believer] you have been called for this purpose, since Christ suffered for you, leaving you an example, so that you may follow in His footsteps." Christ gave us the example of His life so that we followed His footsteps. In Colossians 3:5[169] we read, "So put to death and deprive of power the evil longings of your earthly body [with its sensual, self-centered instincts] immorality, impurity, sinful passion, evil desire, and greed, which is [a kind of] idolatry [because it replaces your devotion to God]." Verse 5 is indicative of verse 2,[170] "Set your mind and keep focused habitually on the things above [the heavenly things],

---

166 AMP
167 NKJV
168 AMP
169 AMP
170 AMP

not on things that are on the earth [which have only temporal value]." Killing a weapon on earth is thinking above and cutting off thoughts on earth. Many people's wars of sin are with action. However, it was the thought that led to the action. When we stop thinking, we stop doing. Our battle is with the idea that is sent to bring about action.

The battle is in thought and not in action. Being overcome by sin shows that we have already been overcome by the idea. This is why James 1:14 says,[171] "But each one is tempted when he is dragged away, enticed and baited [to commit sin] by his own [worldly] desire (lust, passion). Then when the illicit desire has conceived, it gives birth to sin; and when sin has run its course, it gives birth to death." If there is no desire, there is no conception; if there is no conception, there is no birth. When we uproot the root, we destroy the fruit. We stop the flow of water when we block the source. "Come back to your right way of thinking and stop sinning" (1 Corinthians 15:34).[172]

The sanctity of thought precedes the sanctity of life. When I sanctify my thoughts, I sanctify my life. The sin that I did not conquer in the world of thought, I did not conquer in the world of action. Power is not in action but in thought. The potential of action is in thought. Our mind is like a smuggling checkpoint. We hold on to what we don't want to let go of when we deliberately examine and test the idea that came up carefully. Everything we spend without checking is certain to produce trouble in our lives.

171 AMP
172 ERV

Chapter 14—Mind and Discipleship

Matthew 28:19,[173] "Go therefore and make disciples of all the nations [help the people to learn of Me, believe in Me, and obey My words], baptizing them in the name of the Father and of the Son and of the Holy Spirit."

It is very important to understand at least three basic things to live in Christianity:

- *God's free gift (grace)*
  - The grace of God not only saves but also gives a power to live a true Christian life.

- *Believer's gift to God*
  - A change of mind is needed to live the true Christian life, and that is a personal responsibility.

- *Help of the Holy Spirit*
  - Salvation cannot be attempted without the help of the Holy Spirit. It is also impossible to live Christianity without the help of the Holy Spirit.

When the truth of the gospel was enlightened, it changed our insides. But this change is not the only thing that changes us. Our change is given to us so that it goes beyond us and changes others. The main goal of salvation is to become a disciple of Christ on earth. Discipleship is the calling of the converted person to change the world. In Matthew 28:19–20, we are commanded that after a person is saved by the gospel, his greatest mission is to go into the world and preach the gospel to all creation and make disciples.

---

173 AMP

Disciples of the Lord were students of the Lord before they became disciples. He has shown that the manner of life to which they were called to live and learn with Him is not only in words but in the actions of His life. He ordered them to stay in Jerusalem until they received power and to go from Jerusalem to the ends of the earth. In a few years, they flooded the world with the fire of the gospel. They did not have the help of today's technology, but with the power of the Holy Spirit, they preached the gospel to the ends of the earth from sunrise to sunset.

The price paid to them caused them to pay a price. The call to which they were called became the ability to call others. They made the face of the earth, its culture, and even its language spiritual and biblical and changed the history of the world with complete unity and love.

The truth of the gospel saves people. It touches our innermost being and prepares us for a proper spiritual life. However, it is only when we change our mind and have a spiritual mindset that we will have a true and transformed life on earth that honors the Lord. The Lord Jesus gave two clear commandments to His disciples before His ascension: preach the gospel to all creation and teach and make them disciples.

The Two Sides of the Gospel

The gospel has two aspects. One aspect is saving, and the other is transforming. People who are saved by the truth of the gospel have the potential to shake the world. This happens only if they receive the full teachings of the gospel and become a true disciple. If we take note of the Lord's commands, one of them is to preach. Preaching means declaring God's truth in a way that everyone can hear.

This preaching of the gospel is a foolish word. The gospel only saves in the foolishness of the heart and the light of the Holy Spirit. Salvation is God's gracious gift to mankind. This foolish gospel is to accept God's grace by faith that Jesus Christ died for our sins, was buried, and rose from the dead on the third day. No one is saved except by believing the preaching of the gospel. The gospel is not preached to understand but to believe. We cannot explain the gospel to people. When we proclaim, reveal, and preach the gospel with the power of the Holy Spirit, it works, saves, and changes.

The second aspect is very different from the first. Jesus Christ told us to make disciples while baptizing them and teaching them to keep what He commanded us. Teaching to make a disciple and living what we have learned is an absolute commandment.

A disciple must have three basic things to be called a disciple. First is to learn the full teachings of Christ, then have the mindset of Christ, and finally practice living the life of Christ. The goal of our salvation on earth is to be a disciple. A saved non-disciple means a child or a saved worldly person who is not raised and mature. Salvation is the Lord's work. The participation of the believer in salvation is to preach the gospel, but making disciples is the work of the disciples.

Salvation is a one-day event. Like the Lord Jesus, making a disciple is at least three years of work. Salvation is receiving foolish preaching. Discipleship is learning spiritual wisdom and knowledge. One day we stand to receive the Lord, but we become disciples by sitting and learning for many years. Mind renewal is slow and steady. It is not an event; it's a lifelong process.

The apostle Paul said in 1 Corinthians 3:6,[174] "I planted, Apollos watered, but God [all the while] was causing the growth." These three paths of spiritual growth are essential and immutable spiritual laws in a believer. Plantation is one day. When we hear and believe the gospel of truth, we are planted in the kingdom of God. However, the rooted plant only grows if we are watering the plants. Watering is not for one day. It is a daily and life-long work. Once we plant a plant, we don't always plant it by uprooting it. It is important to water the plant we have planted all the time. The Bible testifies that Apollos was an amazing teacher. Paul called this grace of teaching the work of watering. People are planted once by the gospel message. Through education, they are prepared for growth every day. God is the only One who raises.

The issue is clear. We cannot water what is not planted. Raising what is not planted is also impossible. God wants everyone to grow, but if there is no one to water, we will not grow. It is not possible to lead a spiritual life with worldly thinking. As a man thinks, so is he, and the life of a Christian is what he thinks. Renewing the mind of the believer is one of

174 AMP

the most important things in the making of the disciple. Making disciples means changing the mentality of the believer.

When the Lord Jesus was accepted by the people, when His popularity was high, why did He spend time teaching with twelve uneducated people, shaping their thinking, and correcting their lives? He knew that He could turn the world upside down with just a few disciples who sat down and learned and changed their minds.

The Mindset of Christ Jesus

The Lord Jesus accomplished the great purpose that He brought into the world because He had the mindset that He Himself brought with Him. Philippians 2:5[175] says, "Let this mind be in you, which was in Jesus Christ." The NIV says, "Have the same mindset as Christ Jesus." When the Lord came into the world, one of the main things that He brought with Him was His way of thinking. This way of thinking enabled Him to stand firm in the difficult problems of life. Because of this, He went to His Father in complete victory for the purpose of His coming.

At different times and in different ways, the Lord Jesus went through trials and stressful times. Without using His divine power or earthly weapons, He defeated all those who rose and challenged Him. The life of discipleship means being able to change the language, lifestyle, and culture of a society or nation with a changed mindset.

The main challenge during Christ's ministry was not from Satan. Evil spirits were seen worshiping Him or begging Him not to cast them out of people whenever He saw them. It was the Pharisees and Sadducees, who were the religious people, who rose in great opposition and made Him go to His death on the cross. The Pharisees' and Sadducees' great mistake was their incorrect cultural and religious thinking, which went against the Lord Jesus. This was the power that came against the Lord. This is what the Lord won. They opposed Him because of their old culture and traditions. He also resisted them by the new way of thinking and His life of faith.

This was one of the challenges the early church faced when it was founded. The problem with Acts 6 and 15 was unregenerated religious

---

175 KJV

thinking. We do not see Satan challenging and troubling them in any way. However, the culture and mindset that had been ingrained in society for centuries was a big problem even among the saved. In the middle of that great spiritual movement, demons were coming out, sorcerers were surrendering, and many people, including Pharisees and Sadducees, were being attacked and bowed to the gospel. The challenge in their mindset was the culture and system of the old way of thinking. They were the cultural and religious ones who rose to extinguish the torch of the gospel fire that Paul had lit like a wildfire among the Gentiles.

True Disciples Are Agents of Change

When the true disciple's life enters the world with the wildfire of the gospel, it will plant a spiritual and healthy culture in the society's thinking and culture according to God's Word. This is what change means. This is what we should long to see in all our churches today. Today many saved people do not know what the life of a disciple is. Because they do not sit down and learn, they cannot learn to change their worldly thinking and adopt Christian thinking. Even worse, they want the church to be led by worldly thinking.

When the church reaches the world with the gospel and builds a Christian culture with true disciples and the mindset of Christ, then we can say that we have made a real change. Though salvation is a great thing in itself, if salvation does not cause us to change in the world, our Christianity will look like any other religion. Without the power to change the world, there will be no purpose for the church to exist in the world.

Even in the church, the discipleship mentality should be that my brother is more important than me. It is to consider that as one died for all, all should live and die for one. Sacrifice is a way of life, and suffering for the name of Christ is our calling on earth. To humble oneself and elevate others is the daily thought and life of a disciple. Serving others by washing the feet as a servant is the daily thought and life of a disciple. To live is to die, and the Lord is the main and only reason why we live or die. When we carry our own cross and follow Christ every day, then discipleship becomes a reality.

The apostles lost everything. People of whom the world was not worthy were wandering in deserts and mountains and living in caves and holes in the ground. They believed that the world did not deserve them, and they understood that their lives were to serve the generations that had passed and would come. They made their glorious, saved life visible to the world through their sacrifice and blood. Like a city on a hill, they were not hidden, and they exalted Christ. When Christ died for us, we became alive through His death. The calling of the church and every believer should be to make Christ alive and visible in us through our death. This is discipleship. When the self is buried, Christ is glorified. There is no power on earth that can stop or restrain a self-denying person. This is what separates Christianity from other religions. This was the teaching and life of our Lord Jesus Christ. And the order is for us to produce such people.

When this life of discipleship dominates culture, media, language, religion, and politics, Christianity is seen alive. Christianity is said to be lived when this life of Christ enters the family, school, workplace, and business centers of believers. If Christianity is focused only on the service of healing and miracles in church programs, singing, and preaching, Jesus says it will be like putting the light under a bushel basket.

For this reason, the great task of our time is to spread and live the Christian life that the Lord taught us in order to make Christian cultures take root in every business center, politics, media, and society. Below I will try to show a little of what these thoughts are.

The manifestation of discipleship is the ability to live a Christ-like life. But the greatest power that enables us to live this life is that we have a Christ-like mind. Our forefathers strived to live in Christianity and hold this spiritual concept because thinking shapes life. This is why the apostle Paul told the Philippians who paid the price with him in the evangelism in chapter 1:27[176]:

> Only [be sure to] lead your lives in a manner [that will be] worthy of the gospel of Christ, so that whether I do come and see you or remain absent, I will hear about you that you are standing firm in one

---

176 AMP

spirit [and one purpose], with one mind striving side by side [as if in combat] for the faith of the gospel.

He reminds them that unity of purpose and joint or cooperative work is required for them to hear this good news of the gospel. To live according to the gospel of Christ, we should know the gospel requires striving side by side, and then, it requires unity of purpose and joint or cooperative work for others to hear this good news. The work and mission of the gospel also require one mind. The greatest example he gives of this life is the Lord Jesus, and later he urges himself and his other service partners to live this life.

A believer must have a Christ-like mind. Apart from this, the believer does not allow himself to think more or less than he should. Christians should be free from these two mentalities. He shows how we should think by quoting from the example of Lord Jesus.

True Disciples Are the Mark of Love and Unity

In Philippians 2:5,[177] it says, "Let this mind be in you, which was also in Christ Jesus." What was this thought or mindset of Christ? This thinking is the thinking that made Him not count what should be counted. This was when He emptied Himself as a servant to the Father for us while He was equal with the Father and obeyed to the point of death on the cross. This way of thinking cost Him dearly, but it made us in Christ the owner of a life of glory that we do not deserve. When that thought made the master a slave, He made us master. He made us righteous while He carried all our sin. This is what is called the mind of the Lord. Although the life He gave for others cost Him a great price, He brought us to where He was and reconciled us to His Father and made us like Him.

When believers live outside of this, they are caught in the two extremes. First, it raises partiality (selfishness), and second, vain praise (pride). Both are hated by God and prevent us from living true spiritual lives from working in love and unity about the gospel. They hide Christ from appearing in us. In order to avoid these, the apostle raises two contrary suggestions. The first is to be humble, and the second is to think that

---

177 KJV

others are better than us. Humility and thinking that others are more important than us lead to thinking of others rather than ourselves. These things allow us to have one idea and stand together for the gospel.

This kind of thinking brought victory to the Lord Jesus. When He humbled Himself, God caused all creation to bow to Him. Because He served humbly, God exalted Him with the name that is above all names. As He submitted to God's lordship, all creation submitted to Him. His attitude shaped His behavior, and His behavior shaped His life. The apostle's message to the Philippian church was about the attitude they should have in the church. The main purpose of the message is for them to come together in love and to have one mindset that leads to one goal. This is the type of Christ mentality. Unity will not come without changing their thinking. A mind full of selfishness and pride can never come to unity. It cannot live in love. Only a church that has humility and a concern to live for the good of the neighbor rather than for its own good can live in unity and love.

A Thought That We Should Not Think About

The apostle in Romans 12:3 commands that no one think more proudly than he ought to think. For this, it is enough to see his own example. In 1 Corinthians 3:5–7,[178] the great servant Paul talks about himself and Apollos and says, "What, after all, is Apollos? And what is Paul? Only servants, through whom you came to believe as the Lord has assigned to each his task." He says with great humility that they are nothing but assigned to each task. One is for planting, and the other is for watering. In the work of God's kingdom, it is God who makes it grow. When He says we are nothing, He does not mean we have no stake. However, our share is not more than the grace that the Lord wants to use us. A man does not have all grace. Even if it is the grace given to us, it will make us receive the reward from the Lord according to our efforts, but it will not make us better than anyone else. This made them live thinking that they were nothing except for the Lord's grace and what the Lord had done through them.

---

178 NIV

When we think more than we should, we hurt others. When we think less than we should, we hurt ourselves. When we think as we ought to think, we grow ourselves, we benefit the church, we build up the body, we shame the enemy, and we glorify God.

In other words, we can call this the mentality of the body of Christ. When one part of the body says that it is not useful to itself, or if it says that it does not need another part, it harms itself and the body. But when one part of the body thinks that it cannot live without the other parts and the other parts are not complete without it, it gives and receives from others. There will be benefits to other members and others to him. As one lives for the other, he lives for the body. When the body is healthy, it changes its environment. Let us look now at with three thoughts that the Lord Jesus did great work and completely exceeded the Father's will:

- *The spirit of receiving*—He emptied Himself. This is where He completely denied Himself. He received everything from the Father and did nothing of His own accord.

- *The spirit of giving*—this is where He lived with the mindset of a slave. This is a mentality in which He lived only for others without wanting anything from anyone.

- *The spirit of sacrifice*—this is where He gave Himself to die on the cross for others.

The life in which He accepted being completely empty and lived in complete obedience to His Father led Him to live a completely holy life of sacrifice. God emptied Himself and gave Him everything. When He was enslaved, He put all under His feet and caused many to inherit life with Him because of His death on the cross. He did all this, and it happened because of others and us. He honored us. He conquered and made us conquerors.

This is the true life of a disciple. Free from pride and partisanship and living for others. When he gives his own and receives others, when there is a true life that can be seen to all, and when Christianity changes the way of life of the earth, we call this true discipleship. Passing the true life of the Lord Jesus through the culture and tradition of every society, when our true love and oneness are seen and revealed on the outside, and when our being the Lord's makes others jealous of us, this is what we call discipleship. It changes not only the church but the world in Christ's life and His way of thinking.

This is what I call spiritual mind.

ABOUT THE AUTHOR

Pastor Endiryas Hawaz has served as the head pastor of the Minnesota Ethiopian Evangelical Church for twenty-seven years. He is now pastoring in Orlando, Florida. He received an honorary doctorate from St. Thomas Christian University in Jacksonville, Florida. Pastor Hawaz has served the Lord by singing since his childhood and has contributed popular and timeless songs to the glory of God in seven hymn albums for the Ethiopian church. He is the author of the book *The Secret of Wedding and Marriage in Amharic* (Ethiopian language). His teaching on the Word of God is very popular among Ethiopians. He also teaches through live media. He and his wife, Martha, live in Deltona, Florida. They have four children—three boys and one girl.

Milton Keynes UK
Ingram Content Group UK Ltd.
UKHW020940221123
433051UK00020B/1063